Around the Rowan Tree is the sequel to the outstandingly successful **Far from the Rowan Tree**, the story of the Gillies family's brave migration to Canada in the 1950s. Facing the harshness and contrasts of life in the Prairie lands of Alberta, like many immigrants, the Gillieses made out against the odds.

This new book starts on their return to Scotland to life on a farm in the Carse of Gowrie. Margaret Gillies Brown writes simply and movingly about the ebb and flow of life as a farmer's wife with eventually seven children. An inspiring story.

about **Far from the Rowan Tree . . .**

"brilliant insight"
The Big Issue

"you can't help but warm to this"
Farmers Weekly

"pioneers like these are the kind of Scots we should hear more about"
The Local News (Govanhill & Gorbals)

"an easily readable style, the book is an uplifting experience"
Fife & Kinross Extra

"I loved this book because of the atmosphere it creates"
Elizabeth Sutherland

"a heartwarming story"
The Leopard

"compellingly personal, (a) vivid portrait"
Scotland on Sunday

Around
the Rowan Tree

Margaret Gillies Brown

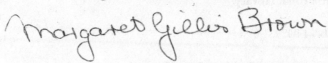

Argyll
publishing

© Margaret Gillies Brown

First published 1999
Argyll Publishing
Glendaruel
Argyll PA22 3AE
Scotland

British Library Cataloguing-in-Publication Data.
A catalogue record for this book is available from
the British Library.

ISBN 1 902831 07 1

Cover Photos   Kathleen Gillies Watt

Origination   Cordfall Ltd, Glasgow

Printing   Caledonian International
Book Manufacturing, Glasgow

To Henry and the family

Oh! Rowan Tree, Oh! Rowan Tree
Thou'lt aye be dear to me
Intwin'd thou art
Wi mony ties o hame and infancy

Scots song
by Carolina Lady Nairne

Hermit Gilliemichael

Hermit – on this low hill
So many centuries ago,
Knowing your brother monks
Were starting to drain the land,
Did you foresee the wilderness beneath you
Rich with grain and grass
And the people fat?

The wide car-rumbling arteries
Or the long yellow-faced monster
Sliding smoothly along steel bands?

Meccano pylons marching single file
to the distant lego town,
The strumming air,

Hill scarred where new pipelines run?

Or were you too preoccupied
Listening for the Voice in the marshes,
Feeling the soul of the world
Rise with the mists in the morning,
Wondering about the quarter moon
Deep soft orange
Like a magnified segment of tangerine
As it tiptoed on the edge of the earth
Before there was a city there?

Foreword

To follow a very successful first volume of autobiography with a second equally successful must always be difficult. Margaret Gillies Brown has achieved this superbly well. I am confident that all the many readers who enjoyed *Far from the Rowan Tree* will be rushing to buy *Around the Rowan Tree*. As for those who have so far missed the first book, they have a treat awaiting them in being able to read two books that must surely become classics of Scottish autobiography. Like Carolina, Lady Nairne, lines from whose Scots song on the rowan tree are given as an epigraph, Margaret Gillies Brown has written books that span a difficult divide – they are both popular and admired as works of literature.

Reading her autobiographies, we may think Margaret Gillies Brown is a woman born under a lucky star. She was fortunate in her parents, with her mother especially important to her. She was fortunate in her first husband, Ronald Gillies, and in the second, Henry Brown; and as this book shows so creatively, she is fortunate in her sons and daughters who have led lives that are almost as interesting as their parents'. She is fortunate to have led an interesting, very varied and sometimes adventurous life. She is fortunate to have been born with a temperament that allows her to face, with considerable courage, what life brings, whilst also, as the modern phrase has it, 'going with the flow'. Her family would not have provided her with such 'good copy' if she had not allowed them the freedom to be themselves, while she and their father provided firm and sound principles by which to live. She has also been fortunate in her publisher.

All these circumstances and attributes are important, but what is more significant is that Margaret was given a natural ability with words. Add to that gift her commitment, over many years, to writing poetry and other works that we learn of in *Around the*

Rowan Tree, and we can recognise something of the means by which she has achieved a masterly use of striking phrases and also the ability to write a very good narrative prose and dialogue. Her autobiographies carry the reader along superbly well; they achieve that most difficult of feats – being 'a good read'.

Margaret has a good eye for landscape and the ability to recognise interesting situations; she also knows, often intuitively, what motivates people and makes them tick. Unlike many writers, she is neither a curmudgeonly woman nor a pessimistic one; she sees the bright side of life rather than the dark although, far from being an escapist who retreats into a sunny world that never can be, she aims to tell it truthfully as she saw it. She does not need, let me stress, to indulge in any unseemly descent into fashionable self-revelations that can be both vulgar and embarrassing.

What finally counts though, is that very obviously, Margaret Gillies Brown is a very good writer. How about this for the first words of a first chapter? '"Well folks, we've made it." The pilot's voice over the tannoy sounded relieved.'

Duncan Glen
July 1999

"

Release came however, one day after an especially worrying time. It was a wonderful Spring day with all the birds singing. I had escaped for a short time and was rambling round the greening fields when in a flash, from nowhere it seemed, words came into my head – ' Thy will be done.'

Suddenly everything tumbled into place. I had been thinking I could solve all the family's problems and bring Ronald back to health. If only I could do the right things, find the right doctors. Now I realised there was only so much I could do, however hard I tried.

Life in the end was in the hands of other forces. I must slacken the reins and live a day at a time, just as I had done in those early days on the lonely prairies of Canada. Tomorrow was unforeseeable.

"

Hard to sing a love song in a storm
When snow-cold gales blow over white Craigowl . . .
from 'Lark Singing in a Storm'
in *Footsteps of the Goddess* (1994)

Chapter I

Homeward Bound

"Well folks, we've made it." The pilot's voice over the tannoy sounded relieved. An enormous red sun had just floated on to the sky as we banked down in the great silver bird towards the Scottish shore. A wrinkled sea lapped the cloud-grey land – home again at last. Ronald and I wakened our sleeping children and saw that their seat belts were fastened. The baby, Grant was still sound asleep in his sky cot. As far as I was concerned it had been a somewhat tense journey.

In Vancouver there had been a delay. "Not quite sure what's wrong with the plane," the pilot had told us, "but we'll see if we can fix it." An hour later, "Well it sure seems okay now." But there was a smidgen of doubt in his voice that left me wondering and we were all in seat 13 too. Not that I was really superstitious but how I would have welcomed at that point a British pilot with his certain assurance and not this laid-back Canadian.

It was 1961 – a miracle people were telling us "fourteen hours from Vancouver to Prestwick over the North Pole." But I was apprehensive. All that was most dear to me, my husband and our five children, here in this plane. We descended at Montreal to refuel – all went smoothly. After a while, once we were cruising through the dark night sky again, seven miles up and heading north over an Arctic tundra, the pilot told us that we would have to make an unscheduled landing at Goose Bay to refuel again.

"Where is Goose Bay?"

"In the middle of Labrador I think," Ronald replied. "Nothing much there but a landing strip cleared of snow."

Half exhilarated, half fearful I waited. It came soon enough with the children still asleep. We thundered down through the freezing air and taxied in. All that was visible through the darkness was flat snow-covered ground, a sparse row of lights, two lonely figures waving paddles and the dim outline of a few tin sheds.

Seven years old, Richard the oldest of the children woke up when the plane's wheels bumped on the hard ground.

"Are we home? Is this Scotland?"

"No Richard, it's Goose Bay in Labrador. We have to come down to take on more fuel."

"But I thought we did that in Montreal."

"We did but it's a long way to Scotland – we need a lot." I tried to let no apprehension creep into my voice.

Richard seemed satisfied with this and interested, he peered out of the window.

"Nothing much here," he said, "but snow and more snow."

Once up in the air again he went back to sleep. Everything seemed to be all right but I couldn't sleep. Here we were flying over ice and snow, mile upon mile of it. I could just see it gleaming in the moonlight below me. Soon we would be home after three long and traumatic years in Canada, first on a Prairie farm and then in the Prairie town of Edmonton where it was nine months winter but had the advantage of sunlight almost every day.

And now Prestwick. The plane taxied to a halt. How very small and inconsequential the Nissan buildings of this Scottish air terminal looked after those of Vancouver. It was a grey day with a slight drizzle but late in October it still wasn't cold. From somewhere I heard a man whistle, a soft cheerful kindly whistle. When I heard that, I knew I was home.

Ronald's father had sent a car to take us back to the farm on the carse land beside the wide River Tay. Dave Scott, farm grieve, was driving as Ronald's father's heart condition rendered him no longer able for such a long journey. It was good to see a kind face. We plied him with questions as he drove through the dreich air. Scotland in one of her sombre moods determined not to put on a show for us but I loved her just the same. It was good to be home.

They were all there to meet us. Ronald's father who had come all the way to Canada in the summer to ask us to come back as he could no longer manage the farm. And my mother and father and younger sister Jean now training for nursing.

Mrs Stockall my father-in-law's plump and cheerful housekeeper had made a huge meal for us – enough for an army. A decent soul needing to be praised over and over again for her efforts. I was too overwhelmed by everything to do it properly. My mother, more than anyone perhaps was ecstatic. Richard had grown so and Michael, the grandson who had missed her the most, six years old now – where had his brown curls gone to? Wee Ronnie was chattering away to her. He had had no recognisable words when he had left for Canada at eighteen months old. And the two she had never seen – Mahri Louise, the one girl in the family, born three months after arriving in Canada, now three years old with fine fair hair and blue eyes and Grant, the baby, nine months – a big strong boy who looked as if he would take life very much as is came making no unnecessary fuss.

"How very small and inconsequential the Nissan buildings of this Scottish air terminal looked after those of Vancouver."

Mother didn't know who to take first on to her knee, although the bigger boys being boys weren't so keen to be cuddled.

Soon it was evening and time for my folks to go over the Tay to their home in Newport before the sailing of the last ferry. Ronald's father had rented a smaller house about half a mile away across the railway and facing the fields of the farm. He and Mrs Stockall departed leaving us all in the large rambling farm house that had once been Ronald's home.

13

Chapter 2

A Place of Your Own

By the time everyone had departed the children were all exhausted but that didn't stop them from exploring the house. How many rooms it had compared with the one we had left in Edmonton. Twenty five in all, Richard counted, if you included the large dairy, washhouse, boot cupboard, coalhouse and pantry. Up a separate stair, leading from the back door, was a large 'maid's' bedroom with a splendid view over miles of fertile fields towards the ever-spreading city of Dundee. At the top of the house, under the steep roof, were spacious attics smelling faintly of apples. This old farmhouse even boasted a small chapel – the newest part of the building. It had been built onto the east wing in 1876 by the local landlord, Lord Kinnaird, when for a few years the Bishop of Brechin had inhabited the house in the last century. On the third landing there was another steep-roofed storey comprising spacious attics.

"Can I have a bedroom of my own?" asked Richard.

"Can I? Can I?" said Michael and Ronnie in unison.

"Now wait a moment, one at a time. Mrs Stockall has sorted things out. You Richard, being the oldest, can have Grandpa's old room looking out to the barn. Michael and Ronnie you can share in the meantime and Mahri and baby Grant will go next to our room." Our room looked out over the River Tay to the Fife hills and Mrs Stockall had borrowed a cot for Grant and put it in there. "How very kind of her," I said, tears coming into my eyes at the consideration of everyone compared with our early beginning in Canada when we had been so very much on our own.

Next morning we woke to autumn sunshine pouring through the wide bedroom window. No one was up yet. The huge sun had just risen over the eastern horizon as I stepped outside into

14

the freshest of air alive with a tingle of frost. How colourful everything was – I had forgotten – the grass vibrant green even at this time of year, the stubble a pale shining gold contrasting with the rich brown shade of the new ploughed land. And how full of detail. How could I ever have thought we were coming back to a flat uninteresting stretch of land? How could the memory have played such tricks? After the flatness of Alberta where we had lived on a prairie farm this was a land surrounded by hills. The Sidlaws rising a couple of miles to the north and to the south the Fife hills stretched for miles and miles. From a tall green fir tree a pigeon crooned and from the oaks in the driveway an unruly crowd of crows, their black wings shining in the sun, were busy looking for acorns. Different sounds above made me look upward. As far as the eye could see the sky was patterned with wavering lines of geese, short lines, long lines and occasionally V-formations, Greylag and Pinkfeet on their way from resting grounds in the river reeds looking for fields on which to graze. I was home.

"Late that evening when the children were all tucked down for the night, Ronald and I had a serious discussion."

Late that evening when the children were all tucked down for the night, Ronald and I had a serious discussion.

"Well, what do you think Margaret? Do you think we should stay here and farm or sell up and go back to Canada?" When Ronald's father had come out to get us he had told us, "The doctor has given me three more years to live. I am retiring – the farm is yours now to do with as you wish. You can sell it and return to Canada or come home and farm it. It's up to you."

"I had forgotten just how much I loved Scotland." I said. "Perhaps you need to go away for a while to realise just how much your home land means to you. Perhaps nowhere else can quite take its place. I would be happy to stay here but what about you? How do you feel about it?"

"Well I've been thinking I would like to give it a try. It could be the wrong decision. If we sold up and went back to Canada

15

it might be possible to make a fortune with the money. Being in Real Estate in Edmonton taught me what terrific bargains there are going in all kinds of property and nobody with the money to buy anything.

"We'll never make a million off farming here but does that matter? What kind of return are we looking for? Uncle Ronnie used to take me round the fields when I was a youngster and show me where all the drains were. He was fascinated by field drains but this land would be useless without them. They are under all the fields and drain into the waterways that the monks began to dig all those years ago – sixteenth century or something. Uncle Ronnie hoped I would farm here. I see that now. He left it to me initially. Did you know that his sisters got him to change his will. My mother bought the other two out and left it to me. Dad had the life rent but no money goes with the farm. We'll have to borrow to begin with which I don't like doing but there's no other way. I won't be able to give you a lot for housekeeping and we've a lot of young ones to feed."

"Don't worry about that," I replied, "I have always had to be thrifty and if Canada taught me anything it was how to be very thrifty. I like it. It's a challenge and perhaps things will get better as the years go by."

"I would hope so." Ronald sounded not altogether convinced. "But farming is always so up and down. There are good years when you think you are making some head way then the bad years come again. It's unreliable but this is a good farm – some of the best wheat land in Scotland. Father just played at farming to a certain extent. A miller to trade, no one knew more about grain than he did but I don't know if he really understood farming. Just as a publisher often would like to be a writer, millers yearn to be farmers. Dad had a big herd of pigs at one time. I looked after them for him. I don't know if they ever really paid. I'm glad he's got rid of them. He used to have a lot of cattle for fattening. But again I think he paid a bit much for them. He liked winning prizes and got the prize for the fattest beast from time to time but was it really worth it? I'd like to change things a bit but it won't be easy with Dad in that house half a mile away watching everything I do. I'd like to simplify things. Do some of the things

I've learned in Canada. Take out a lot of the rotten fences altogether, make wide prairie land that'll be easily worked."

"Well I can help," I said, "like I did at the Shanry Farm before we went to Canada. I liked being assistant shepherd – a pity there's no sheep here."

"No I'm afraid there won't be sheep. Breeding animals are hopeless here – they get too fat on the rich grass. But I won't really need you to help outside and you will have more than plenty to do in the house. Actually we've inherited too many farm workers as it is. We can't really afford so many but I know Dad will not be pleased if I sack anyone. It won't be easy – the old never take kindly to change but change must come. One other thing. An idea that came into my head the other day. Do you think you could cope with another mouth to feed?"

"Who?" I asked hesitatingly.

"Henry."

Henry had been our lodger for a year or so while we lived in Edmonton. Scottish like ourselves he had come back to Scotland recently to attend the wedding of his sister.

"Just a thought," said Ronald, "I don't think he is meaning to return to Canada and he did tell me he would love to start up business here in Scotland if he only had somewhere to start from. It could be a help to him to get him started and he was so helpful to us and I like him. We get on well together. It would probably only be until he got established."

"What sort of business?" I asked.

"Welding is his trade – making things – building – it could be useful here too."

"What's another mouth? Henry would be very welcome. He was no bother and the kids like him. They are a bit short in uncles and he'd make a good one. He could have the old maid's bedroom. It has its own stair near to the back door which would give him a sort of independence."

"That's fine then. I've got Henry's number. I'll give him a ring and ask him to pay us a visit.

Within the next week, just as he had done in Canada, Henry came to live with us.

Chapter 3

Brilliant at Babies

There were many changes within the next five years. Henry left after spending a year with us to go and work on the new Hydro Electric scheme at Loch Awe. However the change that gave me the most joy was the birth of two more children. I had always wanted a large family and two years after we had settled in, Lindsay (called after his grandfather) was born.

"Could I please have the birth at home?" I had asked the village doctor.

"How many babies have you had?" he asked.

"Five . . . this will be my sixth."

"Well nowadays you are supposed to go into hospital after the fifth one but I think I could stretch the rules if you promise that if there's the slightest hint of trouble you will go into hospital."

"Certainly," I said.

"Och I shouldn't say, but I've always thought the best babies are born at home," he retorted.

Dr Edington was new to me but his reputation went before him. "Brilliant at babies," the district nurse had told me. "And loves them – will get up any time of the night. I get into real trouble if I don't call him in time. I'm well qualified to bring babies into the world myself but not long after I came here there was a very straightforward birth to one of the village women. It was the middle of the night. Och, I thought, I won't bother disturbing the doc and my patient thought likewise. What a mistake. I got a real ticking off."

Dr Edington was a smallish squat man with a cheerful face and an easy manner. He was from Glasgow originally and had that humorous easy way with people that many Glaswegians have, treating everyone as if he or she was a close relative. His first name was Robert. In the village he was known affectionately as 'Peel Bob'. He acquired this nickname through regularly handing out to everyone large white pills with M&B imprinted on them. When he wasn't sure what the matter was, if anything much at all, M&Bs were what he gave you, be it for sore throats upset stomachs or nervous disorders. Even his chidren called him 'Peel Bob'. Once when his teenage son was asked what he had been doing that morning, the unexpected reply came,

Dr Edington's way of talking to patients certainly wasn't learned in college.

"Helping Peel Bob to shovel oot a lorryload of M&Bs."

His way of talking to patients certainly wasn't learned in college. But he understood the people and they him. To the stout and cheerful Will who worked in the butchers he would say, "It's like this Will, if you don't give up smoking you're buggered." And to Mrs Nielson, the widow who owned the pub, when she sent up her barmaid to get something for her varicose ulcer, "How can I tell what's wrong with her leg by looking at yours? Tell her to come up herself." When she did eventually come she would tell him that it had been bothering her much of late. "You see I've been busy trying to get the stones off the ground at my new house."

"I've seen you with your barrie and your big backside," he'd tell her. People didn't take offence at what he said. They could understand him and tried to follow his advice. He was particularly good with children, babies and old folk. The latter he visited regularly whether they needed him or not, just to see if they were all right. And children, including my own, pretended to be ill sometimes just to go and see him. He had failings. He would be the first to admit that he was not a good diagnostician. "Funny all my query appendixes have turned out to be pneumonias this year and *vice versa*." Some of his critics said he would make a good vet but on the whole he was loved and I could see me having a happy birth in his care.

It was in the cold month of February that Lindsay was born. In the middle of the night, of course. A fire was burning brightly in the upstairs bedroom. The light was out and strange shadows flickered on the wall. The kindly nurse had elected to stay the night and was dosing by the fire while my great pains came and went. At last the doctor was called. He had asked me earlier if I wanted 'gas and air'. I'd always hoped to try to have the baby without sedation but always been a bit scared.

"Och you'll manage fine without it," he said. "But I'll bring it just in case." And so Lindsay was born unaided but for the doctor's slow unhurried calm instructions. He was an old hand at the game. Knew exactly what was needed and it turned out to be one of my best births. And oh the joy afterwards. Once I was properly seen to and nurse was bathing the baby, Ronald took the doctor off downstairs. Fifteen minutes later he came hopping back singing, *"Cambeltown Loch I wish you were whisky."*

Three years later Kathleen was born in the same bedroom. She was late in appearing – a week late – a fortnight late.

It was October 1967. General Montgomery was visiting Perth. Ronald had very much wanted to be there. "Go," I said. "It won't be today." I felt perfectly all right – too all right!! So off he went. Not long after, the pains started. I waited till evening and then phoned the nurse. At midnight she examined me and said, "A while to go yet – perhaps tomorrow at midday." I'd been having trouble sleeping of late so she gave me a sleeping tablet and with that and her reassuring words I fell fast asleep.

Ronald came in about 1am. I woke momentarily and told him what had happened and what the nurse had said. "I'll not disturb you," Ronald said thoughtfully. "I'll sleep on the sofa downstairs. Here's my stick to knock on the floor if you need me." I woke up about 6am and suddenly knew the nurse was wrong. The birth wouldn't be long. I banged frantically on the floor. Ronald took a wee bit of waking but when he did, dashed upstairs and then was off to collect the nurse. "The quickest way to be sure of getting her," he said.

In no time at all they were back – the nurse and Mrs Hodge, the lady from the village who helped me from time to time. There was nothing she couldn't turn her hand to. She had had seven children herself. One of her children had been premature and had been put in a shoe box by the fire. She had grown to be a beautiful young woman who had seven children of her own, all born at home. Mrs Hodge was a lady of wide experience in that field. Finding the birth imminent they phoned the doctor but baby wouldn't wait and, with the aid of the nurse and Mrs Hodge, came boldly into the world.

Three minutes late the doctor arrived. Very disappointed to be too late. After seeing everything was in order he disappeared downstairs and came back with a cup of tea laughing his head off. "It's the rest of your kids," he said. "They are all half dressed and sitting on top of the Aga." He handed me the tea. "All I can do," he said. It was the worst cup of tea I had ever tasted but I didn't tell him that. It wasn't long before the bedroom was full of people. Ronald and the doc having a dram, the nurse, Mrs Hodge and all the fully dressed children having an apple juice to celebrate this new little girl.

Village Woman
For Mrs Hodge

It's her durability that astounds.
She lives in the echo of hills,
Near run of the pearled river
In a folk-weave village
Skelped by the wind.

She is –
Child bearer,
Housekeeper,
Hen husbander,
Potato picker –
Born to bend into strong breezes.

Now at seventy –
Grandmother,
Great grandmother,
She feels loss if the storm lessens . . .

Looks for more gale
To fight against.

Chapter 4
Time and Tide

Changes were coming gradually to the farm. East Inchmichael had three hundred acres of good arable land. Much of it was sea clay which had been laid down a long time ago. This heavy land could be very difficult to work – plough it or sow it at the wrong time or in the wrong weather and it became unworkable. I remember once Ronald trying to put turnip seed into the ground in late May. "Impossible," he told me. "We had a lovely, fine bed waiting for the seed, then came the heavy rain and now drought and the field's gone as hard as dry concrete – impossible to put seed in that." So that year we had to buy in neeps for the overwintering cattle. The trouble was you could never predict what the weather was going to be in unpredictable Scotland and often your best guess could be wrong and you would get the opposite to what you had expected.

I expect it had always been the same on the farm since first they began to cultivate the land back in the sixteenth century when the monks from Coupar Angus Abbey walked over the Sidlaw Hills looking for the means to more revenue. They were given this useless bit of land bordering the River Tay that was more or less all marsh. They, however, saw potential where no other had and began draining the land by digging ditches, called pows, leading down to the river. Gradually they formed patches of land for possible cultivation. These patches, or pendicles as they were called, were rented out to the people of the Carse. The rent consisted of so much food for the abbey – barley and vegetables from the land and pigeons from the pigeon lofts with their three stone spires, one or two of which are still standing today. Also fish from the stanks. A stank was a pool of stagnant water in which fish were kept and bred, surely the precursor of the fish farms.

On my many walks around the farm I used to imagine how it must have been in those days when the elegant cranes still inhabited the wet land. In my imagination I could picture these delicate-looking, white birds taking off and white wings disappearing into the incredible crimson and gold sunsets we got from time to time. Or I would think of them emerging from the ghostly white mists we still got in the mornings when the ancient hawthorn bushes and willow trees bordering the pows took on strange shapes. During the Reformation one clever abbot, a younger son from some Duke's household, seeing what might happen, gave these pendicles to some of his illegitimate children and so gradually the farms grew.

But the Carse then was an inhospitable place. There were no deep wells and people died of typhoid. There wasn't much in the way of trees – and so wood to make houses was short. The earliest buildings were of clay bound together with horses' hair. It was said of the Carse land, it had neither water in the summer, firewood in the winter nor the grace of God all year round.

Two miles from our farm a village grew where weaving became the main trade until the looms from Dundee took over. Not much was written down about this area so little is known but it was said that once the tents of the army of General Monk were spread over the land.

When sand was being taken from our one hill by those that were making the railway, stone coffins from a much earlier date were found. In the 1980s after an aerial survey in a very dry year evidence was found of a souterrain – a round circle on the ground. So people had lived here on the higher ground from the early time when the Picts had inhabited Dunsinane Hill only a few miles off. There was talk too of a hermit Gillie Michael who was given three acres of land by the local landed gentry. It was a recognised custom to give living space to these holy men who wished to live the life of a recluse. In return the landlord got special prayers for the safety of himself and his family. No one quite knows where Gillie Michael made his clay hut or which were the three acres of land on which he grew his vegetables but I liked to think it was our bit of land called the nine tree brae where the stone coffins had been found. I could imagine him here surveying all the wide marsh land leading down to the river – growing his livelihood on the good free soil, watching the cranes settle as the fine ground-mists cleared.

Why this particular spot was called the nine tree brae we never found out. There were no trees nor any sign of trees having been there but it must have had them at one time.

The rest of the farm was flat. Only the rambling farm house and steading stood on a slight elevation. The whole farm was very compact. Half of it was bounded by the pow draining the land – to the south ran the railway. How often at night I would see those strange steel monsters with dragon gold eyes sweep across the land.

To the west the farm's boundary was the narrow country road that ran up to the village. Only at the bottom of the horse park (called that because it had been the domain of the workhorses of yesteryear) was there a fence between us and our neighbours. This field was permanent pasture where we grazed a few cattle and in the right season gathered the mushrooms that grew in profusion there, still influenced by the past habitation of horses. Because of all those boundaries and few fences we had very few fall-outs with our neighbouring farmers. Their animals did not invade our fields nor ours theirs.

Because the farm was all enclosed like this and compact Ronald took to calling it Fortress Inchmichael inside of which we were all safe. But there is very little real safety in the world I was later to discover. He began to take a great interest in the farm which had been in his family since 1875 and started to implement things he had learned in Canada – the new ideas.

"We must get away," he said, "from the concept of little fields – open it up, get bigger machinery; far more work gets done in less time." So he proceeded to take out fences which were in need of renewing anyway and make wide fields mainly for the growing of barley, wheat, peas and hay. In theory this was fine but the older men, long accustomed to things as they were, didn't take on these new-fangled ideas. They didn't say much but as soon as Ronald's back was turned they were back doing it their way working round the fields that had been. Ronald wasn't a hard taskmaster, often taking and asking advice from the men, but about this he was adamant. Adamant or not the men went their own way as often as not. They reckoned it was less monotonous working their way and therefore as quick.

Not wanting to sack men it was fortunate when the two younger ones left to go to more lucrative jobs outside farming. That left two houses without tenants. The farm had five houses in all, built for workers and their families. In the old days when there were a dozen or so horses and a dairy, they were needed but now we had three empty houses. One was the bothy where the single men lived who were hired in at certain seasons of the year to hoe turnip etc. Now we didn't need them. What would we do with the extra cottages?

"I'm planning low cost farming," Ronald would tell me. "Low in wages which are ever increasing. It will be high cost in machinery – a bigger combine, bigger tractors to pull bigger implements – and most important of all a grain drier of our own. Father used the grain dryer belonging to the business he had once owned but I can't do that so readily. Anyway, sometimes at the crucial moment, you have to wait in the queue until you get your grain dried – a waste of precious time."

I went along with all that he said only too pleased to see him happy.

"We will still grow peas I think, a good break crop and Smedley needs plenty for his canning factory in Dundee. Besides we're all equipped for that."

Opposite the bothy stood the pea viner which we shared with a neighbour. We had all the equipment needed to cut and harvest peas. "We'll do away with the hens, I think," said Ronald. We had a big hen house and run, with three hundred hens. This was my domain. I fed the hens, collected and washed the eggs. Hens were usually the wife's responsibility and where she got her pin money – extra for clothing the children etc.

"Hi, what about my pin money?"

"I've thought of that but hens are not really economical any more. Now that farms have started with battery hens in thousands. I don't like the idea of that. We'll keep a few hens for our own use but the rest will go."

"But my pin money?" I persisted.

"I've thought of that," Ronald repeated. "We've three empty cottages now. We can rent them out and you can have the proceeds. It won't be all that much. If you ask anything much in the way of rent it gets hugely taxed as unearned income. The houses will be easy enough let. The problem is, if we should change our farming policy and need them for again for workers we could be in difficulty. Once people have made a home it's hard to get them out. I'd hate to evict anyone who didn't want to go."

"I think I may have the answer to that," I said. "I was speaking to Mrs Redford at the station the other day. They had a house surplus to requirements and they've let it out to students from Dundee University. Seemingly there is a great shortage of student accommodation and the organisers are happy to get anything. Students will always go when their studies are over."

And so it was settled.

I approached the university. They sent someone out to see the cottages and approved and I spent a busy time furnishing them with everything I could think of that students might need. Nothing was too expensive so that it wouldn't matter if things got broken. With some help I painted up the houses – they were ready when our first boys arrived.

They became like sons to me – interesting elder sons who would be doctors, lawyers or teachers. I could have interesting conversations with them on things outside farming. Also later on one or two became very useful for coaching children that were averse to scholastic work as most of mine were. Students fitted in well with the farm. They always paid their rent quarterly as soon as they got their grants. They were all decent boys – pleased to be out in the country, usually owning an old banger which was always giving trouble. When I think of those students I think of them either inside studying or outside with long legs stretching out from under old jalopies.

Chapter 5

Hearth and Home

The kitchen was the heart of the home – by far the most used room. It was a large farm kitchen with a smaller scullery off. Ronald's parents had come to live at Inchmichael in the middle of the war after the death of uncle Ronnie. Ronald's mother had insisted on the house being done up. It had fallen into disrepair during the years when the unmarried uncle Ronnie had lived there with a housekeeper. There was woodworm in the attic and the chapel at the far end of the house had been used as a tattie store. The farm belonged to Ronald's mother but it was his father, the grain merchant, who wanted to run the farm and live on it.

"I'll easily do that as well as look after the grain business," he told her. "In fact it will fit in well to have a farm. I'll come to know the problems of the farmers better and the difficulties of getting good samples of grain."

So his wife agreed on condition that the house be renovated.

"I'm not leaving a comfortable town house to freeze on a farm."

Probably much more money was spent on the house than they could afford but I became everlastingly grateful to her for the improvements that she had made particularly in the kitchen. The old stone flags had been removed and in their place the most durable of green and brown bitumen tiles put down. Also an enormous second-hand Aga was installed with four ovens and a huge stove at the far end for heating water. The result was that the kitchen was never cold with the stove on night and day for nine months of the year. The kitchen faced west and had a big window with small panes. It faced on to the large farmyard boxed in by old red sandstone cow byres, stables, outhouses of all sorts – no view but I thought the old buildings rather beautiful especially when a westering sun sank its rich red tones into the

27

pantile roofs. It was handy, as I could see what was going on around the farm and it was also the place where the children played, racing round on their bikes, playing tig or hide-and-seek, cowboys and Indians, chasing each other with water pistols. Beside the garden wall a load of sand was dumped. Here the smaller ones would play happily for hours when the weather permitted. However the farmyard wasn't the safest place in the world especially at busy times when tractors would come racing in with grain. You had to keep a watchful eye on the children.

The kitchen also had several large cupboards and a long pine table against one wall and another antique table ruined, some would say, by a Formica top, in the alcove in the window. This was the oldest part of the house. Here the walls were about three feet thick and made from a mixture of clay and horse hair. The adjacent scullery faced east. It could have had the most magnificent view of the long green valley stretching to the distant city on the horizon had not Ronald's mother put in opaque glass to prevent, I suppose, the maid looking out and being distracted from her work by the men on tractors coming along the farm road looking in. It was many years before there were changes. I just accepted things as they were.

However I did get a joiner to make benches to use at the pine table where we ate most of our meals. The reason was there was always an expanding amount of children especially on Saturdays and in the school holidays when my children asked down their friends from the village. It was two miles to Errol. Far too far, I was always told, for their friends to go back for a meal. Please, please could they stay. So meals became expandable especially on Saturdays when mince became the order of the day. If I found I was going to be short I could always add cornflour and more Burdles Gravy Salt. Once I remember being really short of food in the house in the days before I had a freezer.

"But I don't have enough food today boys, I really don't. Colin'll have to go home. He's got a bike. The only other thing I've got is a tin of figs."

At this there was some consulation between the boys and then Richard said, "Colin likes figs." So Colin stayed and ate a whole tin of figs without apparently coming to any harm.

But it wasn't only children who filled the kitchen. Everyone was entertained there – neighbouring farmers, salesmen, even on rare occasions the minister and if it got to meal time and discussion was still in progress another place or two was laid at the table. There were always huge pots of soup on the Aga and I could always rustle up something.

All sorts of different people, as time went on, would appear in the kitchen. One man in particular that I remember was the Piano Man. I can't recall his real name as we always called him the Piano Man. Once a year in July he always arrived unannounced to tune the old pianola that he'd fallen in love with. A man of indiscriminate age he had the look of a rather absent-minded professor. Rather squat in stature he wore an old brown tweed jacket which sat on him comfortably and went well with his calmy smoking pipe. He came in an old car, a bit bashed about, that certainly would not have passed its MOT today. He spent most of the day with us. First of all the plinks and plonks of the tuning of the piano could be heard through the house and then lunchtime. Ronald brought out the whisky bottle and a large measure was poured out for him. All through lunch you could see an amused smile on his face.

At that time of year it was always a packed table as it was holiday season. Sometimes the kids were an unruly bunch. Ronald sat at the head of the table. He could keep order quite easily if he wanted. One word of warning from him and they were quiet but he had a way of treating the children like adults and some discussion would arise which might get quite heated. The Piano Man never said much just smiled but one day said to me, "I can't help thinking of the film Seven Brides for Seven Brothers when I come here." After lunch there would be a bit more plink plonking at the piano and then unasked we would get the most wonderful recital for about half an hour or so after which he was gone until next year.

Unfortunately we were not a musical family but Mahri-Louise, from an early age, showed a predisposition towards music and at three could play simple tunes by ear. I always wondered at that because even to this day I can't make two notes work at all.

Perhaps my favourite music was always the natural sounds –

29

the sound of wind and sea, the rustle of ripe barley, birdsong and especially the song of the canary which I always had in the kitchen in a cage hanging in the window.

Canaries were supplied to me by an old man from the village, Sam Cairns. He and his wife were neighbours of Mrs Hodge who came to give me a hand for a few hours once a week.

The Cairns had thirteen children, the Hodges seven. In the early years when things were tough for them with so many mouths to fill, food was often shared across the fence. If Ma Cairns had soup left over it was passed over and vice versa. Nowadays Sam was retired but worked as a petrol pump attendant up in the village probably to get enough money to feed his canaries. He had the same deep love for them as the Piano Man had for music.

"One that sings, please Sam," and he would always give me of his best. So much so that sometimes the canaries drowned out the other noises in the kitchen. The more noise there was the louder they sang. Sometimes Ronald would say, "Shut that damn bird up," and I would have to put a cloth over the cage in the hope that this would stop it.

They were busy days, the kitchen days, but happy ones. Some seasons of the year they were busier than others. In summer I made a lot of jam with raspberries, strawberries, plums and apples from garden and orchard. For me there's no better smell than the aroma of raspberry jam unless it is the smell of bubbling plum chutney. A lot of the time was spent in cooking and baking to feed hungry mouths but it was something I loved doing and I couldn't quite understand this new upsurge of women's talk about drudgery in the kitchen – that we must go out and do something valuable and creative with our lives. What was more valuable than feeding a family? What was more creative than making the most out of the foods available? So happily I made pigeon pie and jugged hare, baked scones, rockcakes, pancakes. And my reward? – to see happy well-fed children and have someone come into the kitchen and say what a glorious smell! What's cooking?

Chapter 6

Home Help

"You will need to get a girl to help you in the house," Ronald said one day not long before Lindsay was born.

"I'll easily manage," I said "Remember I looked after seven children under seven years old when we were in Canada."

"But you also have this big rambling house to see to. You know I have often said it killed my grandmother and it killed my mother who was found lying in the dairy one morning having had a stroke. Her children were grown-up and away and she had more help than you. That's where we'll find you if you don't do a bit less."

"Your mum was a perfectionist – kept the house like a palace – regularly wiped away all the cobwebs beneath the pictures – I'm afraid I'll never be a perfectionist, Ronald. Housework and palaces don't interest me enough. Besides in the short time I came here before your mother died, you felt frightened to rumple a cushion or raise your voice much above a whisper let alone muddy the floor. I don't want to have a home like that. I want the children to have freedom to shout if they want to and not always be afraid of making a mess."

"Well I think you've certainly achieved that," Ronald laughed and tried a different tack.

"Speaking from a selfish angle I need you more, Margaret, now that we have fewer men on the farm. Already you spend a lot of time answering the phone and the door, entertaining salesmen but more and more during the busy time especially, you're very handy for running to get a spare part, extra seed or whatever."

Reluctantly I was worn down and so Catherine came to us. Catherine was eighteen and pretty enough in an unstartling way even if she looked sulky most of the time. I can't remember how I heard of her. But what I do remember is going into Dundee and being grilled by nuns to see if I was a suitable person, being non-Catholic, to employ one of their girls. I must have passed the test and Catherine arrived. Catherine was quite a competent worker and did lighten my load a bit but she was a town girl with no great love for children which after a while began to show. In a way she had a dual personality – reasonable enough most of the time but when her bus driver boyfriend phoned she completely changed. It was down tools and off as soon as she possibly could. I have never in all my life seen someone get ready to go out as quickly as she did. Straggling hair became a small stiff beehive. Jumpers and blouses were washed and dried with a hair drier and she was off in fifteen minutes transformed. Apart from that the house rang with songs from a loud record player she carried around with her. *Return to Sender* was played over and over again. It must have been her favourite song and it wasn't long before I was feeling like returning her to sender. The crunch came however a week before Lindsay was due to be born when I had had to go an urgent message. When I returned I found Mahri, now four, and Grant, two, left in the house alone. She was off with her boyfriend. That was no use to me at all. There was a row and she was gone.

The next attempt came about six months later in the summer months when I was incredibly busy. We were now growing raspberries which involved a lot of extra work. A friend phoned one day.

"Margaret, I've got a couple of au-pairs from France here for the summer, I only really need one. I know how busy you are. Would you like one?" Francette was very different from Catherine – petite and pretty, unable to speak much English, a student accustomed to academic work rather than physical, she needed time spent with her which I didn't have. She hadn't much discipline over the older boys. They used to tease her unrelentingly at the table because she wanted to eat nothing except lettuce and lemons. Watching Francette eat lemons seemed to fascinate the boys but also bring out the worst in them. We used to take Francette with us when we went out. On one rare occasion we had a meal in a country hotel. There were other farmers there that we knew. We got talking. One was especially curious about Francette.

"She's from France, can't speak much English," Ronald told him.

"My God she's thin," he said, "must have been the one on the blind teat." I loved the way farmers brought things back down to earth. No way would Francette have understood what he was saying as he spoke in Scots and no way would she have known that mother pigs often have an extra teat that provides no milk. When they are newly born each piglet finds his own teat and sticks to the same one each time he feeds. No other piglet is allowed to touch it. If they are too many piglets one lands with the blind teat and has to steal what it can from others and therefore never thrives.

> When I got back in the evening there was an eerie silence. Immediately I knew something was wrong.

I didn't leave the children in Francette's care until one day I got an SOS from my mother. Father was haemorrhaging at home in Newport across the river. Ronald was at a sale. I asked Francette, "Do you think you will manage?"

She nodded assent. I spoke with the boys.

"You have to be especially good," I said. "Your grandfather's ill. Don't give Francette a hard time. She's in charge."

With these instructions I left. When I got back in the evening there was an eerie silence. Immediately I knew something was wrong. There was no one about and then round the corner came Richard.

"It's David . . . " he explained haltingly.

"David? What's he doing here?" David was thirteen.

"He came to play with us this afternoon and we went down on our bikes to the pea fields and David ate an awful lot of peas and, and . . . "

"And what?"

"You know that cupboard where you keep the drinks when you have a party."

"Yes."

"Well David found it and drank half a bottle of vodka."

"And what about the rest of you?"

"No we didn't."

I didn't think they would. They had far too healthy a respect for what their father would say to them.

"Where's David now?"

"Round in the garden trying to be sick."

Just at that moment Ronald drove into the yard.

Quickly I told him what had happened. With immediate presence of mind Ronald stuck his fingers down David's throat. The boy came to a bit and with a great convulsion out came what looked like a thousand peas. I left David with Ronald and went to phone the doctor.

"Where's Francette?" I asked Richard.

"She's locked herself in her bedroom. I think she's frightened of us."

The doctor arrived quickly and soon David was off to hospital.

Chapter 7

Jane

It was a year or so before I ventured to think of trying again for a girl in the house.

"Never again," I had said to myself and now Ronald didn't press the point.

And then one day I got a phone call from another farmer's wife I only knew vaguely. She had heard that at one time I had been looking for a girl to help with the children. "Do you still need one?" she asked. "I help out in a voluntary capacity in a children's home. We have a girl that is looking for work. She is a good girl and we would like to see her settled and happy. Could you help? She would be half foster child and half home help. If it didn't work out, we would take her back. She's fifteen. We've tried her in a few jobs but they were all in the city and she just didn't like them. She's a country girl at heart. Her father works on farms. Her mother became ill when the girl was very young and has been in a home ever since. What do you think?"

"Well," I was hesitant over the phone. "I do need someone at the moment and I've always had an interest in fostering. Can I phone you back? I'll discuss it with my husband."

I was at the time feeling rather stressed out with overwork. Mother and father both came to stay with me for a while – both invalids. They wouldn't be staying for ever but I was feeling under the weather. Also, secretly, ever since being in Canada and looking after three children not my own while there, I had entertained the idea of looking after foster children. I thought perhaps I had the ability for it. I could make a difference to their battered lives and yet be able to let them go when the time came. But when I suggested it to Ronald, some time after we came back, he had said emphatically, "No. You can have more of your own if you like but no foster children."

Here was my chance.

"I've got an offer of a girl to help me in the house," I said to Ronald that evening.

"I thought you said, never again."

"I did, but this one . . . " and I explained to Ronald all that Mrs Pilcher had told me leaving out the bit about fostering.

"Well you can but try. You certainly need someone."

And so Jane came to us. On the first visit she came with a social worker.

"We'll bring her down every weekend for a month or so to see if it works," she told me but Jane would have none of it. She immediately took to Inchmichael, knew this was where she wanted to be and so her second visit was for keeps.

"Willing," the social worker told me, "but wearing." This, to begin with, turned out to be a fairly accurate description. She was a pretty girl with masses of dark curls and rosy country cheeks. Her eyes were bright as the sunrise and a smile never far away. She had in all a cheerful countenance which completely belied the difficult childhood she had had. There was no chip on her shoulder anywhere to be seen. The past was the past. She was big now and a whole new life was stretching out in front of her which she meant to get on with and enjoy to the best of her ability. On her first visit she had not been a particularly prepossessing figure. Straight from the children's home she wore knee length white socks which would have reached to her knees had they not been at different wrinkly levels. Her unbecoming skirt hung at different levels too, drooping at the back and shorter at the front due to her being a little plump about the waist. After some time with us she slimmed down, got herself some clothes of her own choosing and became a presentable young teenager.

She was a quick learner and in some ways seemed to be fearless. On the few times she elected to go to town she walked to catch the main road bus half a mile away. She always took a lethal-looking hat pin with her. "Pity the poor man that tampers with her," I thought to myself. Not that ever anything did happen on these quiet country roads that our own children were often on also.

"Let them walk or get on their bikes," Ronald would say to me when our lot wanted to go up to the village. "It's not good to pamper kids over much, they've got to learn that the world doesn't owe them a living. Besides, you haven't time to run them here there and everywhere at their demand."

Ronald's word was law and we all accepted without demur. I realised, in later years, how often he had been right.

In some ways, in the most important way, Jane came to me like an angel from heaven. She was totally responsible with the children and kind to them. I found quite soon I could leave her in charge. Nothing on earth would have ever made her leave them and she would guard them with her life. They weren't the easiest children to deal with either – all of an independent character and all determined in their own ways but she had a nice cajoling way of dealing with them – and got through to most of them. The older boys rather resented her to begin with. Richard saw her as not much bigger than himself and who was she to tell them what to do. But she managed to get a pact with him. And so he would help her.

Michael was the difficult one. He teased her unmercifully as he did his younger brother and Mahri-Louise. He was the one that was likely to get in the most mischief also. Who was it broke the branch of the plum tree? The barn window? Who was it that scattered stones on the grass that broke the mower? It wasn't always Michael but because it usually was, he always got the blame. Jane never got cross at him. Rather next time she paid a visit to the milk bar she would buy a poke of sweets just for him. Oddly at the age of fourteen Michael's attitude to life completely changed and he became one of the easier boys to manage but by that time Jane was gone.

Michael wasn't the only one to tease Jane. She was easily teased and a pleasure to tease as she made a great good-humoured fuss about it. One or two of the farm workers loved to tease her. One day she came bounding into the house in high indignation.

"Look, look what I've found," she said holding up a poster of a bare naked lady.

"Where did you get that?" I asked.

"It was pinned above my guinea pig cage." (I'd given her a guinea pig for her birthday after she'd told me how she would have liked a pet of her own as a child but had never got one and how she would like one of her own right now.)

"I bet that was Jamieson," she said tears of annoyance in her eyes, which soon turned into laughter.

From time to time she loved to have a laugh with the men on the farm. Once, at pea harvesting time, when there was a lot of bustle round at the pea viner, she came running back to the house.

"Mrs Gillies, Mrs Gillies."

"Whatever's wrong?"

"It was Joe."

"What did he do?"

"He gave me a sweet and it was only a bit of chalk."

"So."

"I ate it and didn't realise until they told me!!"

Jane's housework wasn't of the best but then I wasn't the best of teachers on that subject. Not like my mother-in-law who had treated maids quite differently. I was told she certainly wouldn't have given them birthday gifts and let them off with things the way I did. She was hard on them, taught them properly, was impervious to tears but they used to come back years later and say what a good boss she was. I suppose I wasn't cut out to be a boss really and knew it.

Jane stayed with us for three never-to-be-forgotten years but she began to get restless and wanted pastures new. She left and went down to England where she stayed for several years having several jobs before becoming nanny to a wee boy of a famous actor. After he went to school she came back to Scotland, married and had two children of her own. I still see her from time to time. She hasn't changed.

Chapter 8

Into the Raspberries

Ronald's father, old Lindsay, died a month after young Lindsay was born. Secretly we knew he was pleased at Lindsay's birth – plenty Gillieses to carry on the name. But it wasn't everyone's reaction.

"Not another one," other relations had said. "In this over-crowded world what are they all going to do when they grow up? The farm won't keep all of them." After having spent three years in the wide open spaces of Canada this thought didn't worry me over much. There, children had been welcome and wanted. And they got free fares on the bus I remembered. Every encouragement was given for you to have more.

Also, in these days, when I had little time for reading and a women's magazine was about all I could get through, I read a serialised story which influenced me a lot. It was a true story and the author was going for a dozen children and had reached the halfway mark. She hadn't much money or anything, took in lodgers etc. and managed. It was a happy story – could it be mine? What if I was criticised – I didn't need to listen. What was the saying – "they say, what do they say – let them say."

It was a sad day for all of us, old Lindsay's passing, but as far as he was concerned it was a blessing in disguise. He was over eighty and had not kept good health for quite some time and had agreed to go in to a nursing home a couple of days before he took the massive heart attack that killed him. How he would have hated being totally dependent on nurses.

On the way to Canada, when he came out to talk to us, he had taken ill on the ship, landing in hospital and after a thorough examination he had asked the doctor, "Tell me doctor, how long have I got? Tell me the truth."

"Three years at the most," was the reply and it was almost

three years to the day that he died. In a way, I think these were three happy years for him. He was getting on better with Ronald, his son, than he ever had before and he loved having his grandchildren so near. He loved children, especially those that didn't argue with him, with one exception – young Ronnie, who did argue with him. Not long after returning from Canada I happened to look out the window to see grandfather and grandson at the age of four in combat.

Grandfather was shaking his stick with rage and wee red-haired Ronnie was jumping up and down in equal rage. I never did find out what the conflict was about but from that day forth they became firm friends. Why, I'm not quite sure. Perhaps they realised they had both met their match. Perhaps grandfather saw himself again in Ronnie and from then on Ronnie would, several times a week, get off the school bus early and go for his tea with his grandfather. He and Mrs Stockall spoiled him outrageously but the others never objected. They were a little nervous of their grandpa and it seemed Ronnie didn't know what fear was.

After he died, Mrs Stockall now well over sixty, married her beau of eighty and they went to live in a caravan. We used to visit them sometimes. What a pretty bright place – full of singing canaries that were allowed to fly free and the many nicknacks that Mrs Stockall had gathered over the years. When she died, not so many years later, she was still in hospital about to be sent home after a heart attack. The nurses told us, "She died laughing."

When we visited her widowed husband some time later we expected to see changes and a disconsolate man – not so. Nothing much had changed in the caravan – the nicknacks were still all there and the canaries singing and flying around.

"She's still here," he told us smiling. "Come and see this." He took us over to the small dresser crammed to overspill with treasures. Bang in the centre was a huge ornate wooden casket.

"She's in there," he said. "All of her."

She was a big lady.

The death of Ronald's father put us further into debt. Although Ronald had inherited the farm, the movables belonged to his two sisters – implements, crops etc. We would have to borrow more to give them their dues.

"We'll have to find another crop that will bring us in a bit more money," said Ronald one evening. But what?

"What about something in the fruit line," I suggested. "The Carse of Gowrie used to be famous for its fruits."

Ronald agreed. Carse of Gowrie, tap of the tree, the street vendors used to shout in Edinburgh but there are no apple orchards left to speak of. Besides other places can grow them better and so many apples are imported these days."

"How about strawberries," I said. "Remember your father grew half an acre of them once. Boy, they were beauties."

"Yes but remember the weeds and the slugs – I've never seen such weeds. It really would be a high cost crop."

"Raspberries then. What about raspberries?"

"Everyone says you can't grow raspberries in the Carse. They of all fruit need well-drained soil."

"Who's everyone?" Ronald thought a moment.

"Well the farmers in Blairgowrie district mainly, who grow so many on their sloping well-drained fields."

"Perhaps they don't want us to start growing them down here – don't want to encourage competition."

"Raspberries are a possibility." Ronald was becoming enthused. "Instead of having to buy extra heavy equipment I could make the drills wider than normal and use the farm equipment. They could go in the station field – the land's a bit lighter there. We won't get a crop for three years but it's worth a try."

And so we went into raspberries which became, for a time, a lucrative crop. As far as I was concerned it was more than a lucrative crop, it was a useful crop, an enjoyable crop. It gave the children something to do in the long summer holidays. Because to begin with we were the only people in the district growing raspberries we had the people of the village to call on for help and they came in their droves with their children in tow. Sometimes young mothers came wheeling prams from the village two miles away. The children didn't all pull their weight. They would pick for a while and then grow tired of work and start berry wars – throwing berries at each other till they were shouted at by their mothers or the gaffer. Ours were no exception apart from Kathleen, who at the early age of three liked picking berries or was it perhaps the pennies poured into her hot sticky little hands that was the chief incentive? For the children of the village it helped to pay for their school uniforms and shoes – was a help to the whole family.

Sometimes for no particular reason we would be short of pickers and I would go down to the berry field to pick also. I loved those days. I can remember them yet. Contrary to what we had been led to believe the berries grew thick and huge and were easily picked. The smell was entrancing in the hot showery afternoons, hidden in amongst the berry canes which kept you sheltered from any wind there might be. The overheard snatches of conversation through the thick green leaves could be intriguing and then at last when you were getting a bit weary the gaffer shouted from the weighing cart, "Berry up" and the invisible people hurried up the green aisles to get their berries weighed for the last time that day. Red-stained hands, money hot to the touch, happy tired children. All that is more or less gone now with the new raspberry-picking machinery.

Sometimes students came and asked for a job berrypicking. I can remember one occasion particularly well. There was a mixture of young men and women lost among the leaves or so we thought. One sultry afternoon Ronald was alerted by a continuous whistle from a train as it passed. He went down the field to investigate and found at the bottom of a drill one of the pretty young girl students picking away at the raspberries, topless.

"Good God, lassie," said Ronald, "you'll need to put some clothes on. "Did you not hear that train hooting as it passed?"

"Why?" she challenged him. "I'm hot. In France when picking grapes I used to do it all the time."

"This is Scotland – no France," was his reply.

42

Chapter 9
Unwillingly to School

When they were young the children went to the village school. Fortunately the village was just within the distance for a school bus to collect them. Any nearer and they would have had to walk or bike to school. I don't think Ronald would have had me pandering to them by running them to school in the car. "Waste of petrol," he would have said. "It's good for them to walk." And in these days the country roads were quiet.

It wasn't until Lindsay and Kathleen, the last two children, came of age that there was any playschool. To go to playschool for a few mornings in the week did make a difference. It was a good introduction to school and by the time they did go they knew the children they would be mixing with. Before playschool days I always had a bit of trouble to begin with. Always they would escape and walk home from school at least once, saying now that they had been to school they weren't going back. Grant, the boy who was born in Canada, had the record for this. The first day of going to school he walked back three times. I immediately took him back by car. There was nothing really wrong and he had to go to school. Of all the children he was perhaps the most stubborn. We hadn't particularly noticed because he was so docile a child and didn't get mixed up in fights like the others. He wasn't phased by Michael's teasing – took life calmly. He didn't however take to school until he was in his third year and got a teacher that with her different methods of teaching got through to Grant's imagination and he began to see there was some reason for schooling after all.

In the days before playschool some of the farmers' wives got together and had coffee mornings in each other's houses. This was a good idea as the young wives had an enjoyable exchange of news and ideas and the children enjoyed different toys. There were lots of squabbles among the toddlers of course. It's always a difficult business, learning to share.

The village school had just over a hundred pupils. It had a teacher for every class except the top one and this the headmaster took himself. This he always resented, finding it difficult to do both jobs and often he was forced to be absent from that class. As a headmaster Ronald and I liked him. He had the same ideas as us about education. It was important but the top priority was the happiness of the children and trying to bring out the best in them – an all-round approach. After all, they had only one childhood. It wasn't a rehearsal. It seemed, in some ways, that he hadn't quite grown up himself and enjoyed being among all the children. He understood them so was able to sort out squabbles with little fuss, great consideration and fairness. Football for the boys was important. It was fun and every child should learn to swim, so he arranged a weekly jaunt to Perth to the swimming baths. Once a year children from the two top classes had the offer of going to London with him and a couple of other teachers.

Getting all of them off to school in the morning was always a struggle – getting the sleepyheads up in time to get a good breakfast and find missing schoolbags etc. Finding matching socks was the worst – so many orphan socks. Did the washing machine, an old Bendix that my mother-in-law had used, eat them? But at last they were all off and quietness reigned in the kitchen for short while.

In the evenings they brought home their school lessons. Fortunately they didn't have all that many. Just as well, because Ronald's attitude to home lessons was the children worked all day at school, that should be enough – and they of course agreed wholeheartedly with him. There were always so many interesting things to do on the farm – never a dull moment. They helped at the busy times with hay, peas or the raspberry harvest, although Ronald never insisted that they should work. Until they were sixteen they were not allowed to drive a tractor contrary to what some farmers' sons were. But there were games to play with the village boys, cowboys and Indians, space wars, water wars with squeezy bottles and water pistols and on one occasion dung wars – a very smelly affair when they had all gone into the horse park and flung cows' dung at one another. To my horror I found Ronnie had used my butter clappers to scoop the stuff up with. Then there was fishing in the pow (although they never caught much) and shooting with an air gun – learning to drive a car round the old farm road. Endless the hours of adventure and fun in the long summer days.

In the winter time they spent a lot of their evenings in front of a warm roaring fire curled up watching telly. It would have been a thought going out of the warm living room with its thick old velvet curtains and winking coppers to switch on the electric in their cold rooms and do home lessons. You would have had to be a dedicated learner and not one of them was. We didn't help, I suppose. Ronald hadn't enjoyed his school days – said he had learned everything after he left school. And indeed he was a great reader with a most retentive memory and knew so many things that often the boys would not need to open up an encyclopaedia for information, just ask Dad.

Myself, I had hardly been to school as a child, always pleading poor health (fairly justified). My vivacious mother, an MA and college-trained teacher, taught me when she had time but books fascinated me and I had read voraciously when young. Then at eighteen I had applied to the local hospital for training as a nurse. After a half hour's interview with the matron I had been accepted and after three years got my SRN. I remembered no particular difficulty with the exams. I had, at that time, been dedicated to passing and used to get up at five in the morning to study.

However when the children began to filter to the new comprehensive schools in Perth, Ronald and I recognised a changing world in which because of threatening widespread unemployment, passing exams – gaining a paper qualification – was becoming important.

"They can't all be farmers," Ronald would say. "This farm won't support more than one the way farming is today. I do wish we could do other things from the farm. But what? I'm sure there is potential here."

Our exhorting them to learn perhaps came too late. We had set up a state of independence in their minds. We had also

45

however told them that there was nothing they couldn't do if they really wanted to. I had been told this by my mother from an early age and I was female. I was never told there were things women couldn't do, so never had hang-ups about male domination. The only trouble with our children was that they didn't want to do anything very much. As far as they were concerned all the necessary politics of life went on in the Errol school bus that took them to Perth. Mostly the boys' biggest ambition was to leave school and become lorry drivers, farm workers or gamekeepers. They wanted to leave – get on with life – get a job. But we did insist that our boys got as many exam passes as they could. Then they could always go back to education at a later date if they found they needed to.

I haven't mentioned the girls in all this but then it was a boy's world. Mahri-Louise grew up a quiet pretty little girl but not very clever at school. In fact the first teacher (unfortunately not a good one) reported that she was unteachable. This was in the days before we got the new headmaster and there was no help or hope from the old one.

I happened to know a young teacher, just left college, who couldn't wait to become a teacher. The summer before she started work, she came out to teach Mahri – tried every method, found what was most suitable for her and taught her to read.

However Ronald was so incensed at the uncooperative attitude of the village school at that time that he insisted she went to a private school.

"We'll put her to Craigclowen," he said, "we'll afford it somehow." And so Mahri-Louise at the age of six had to catch the bus at 8 o'clock for Perth. She was happy there with the extra attention, and learned.

Kathleen – the youngest was a completely different sort of girl – red-haired and lively, she just seemed to grow. I hardly remember her childhood. Being brought up largely by boys she became like them and wouldn't have dared tell tales on any of them, how they skived off school etc. She grew up perhaps with the same rebellious nature – lessons? what were lessons? But she enjoyed her schooldays, was outgoing, unafraid of the world.

46

Chapter 10

By Loch Rannoch

Holidays were always taken in June. "It has to be that month," Ronald would tell me. "I must be back for the hay."

"But it's still school term," I would mildly object.

"Farmers can't run their schedules by school terms. Besides, they'll be off shortly and in the last few weeks of school, as far as I can see, there's not much work done."

The new headmaster never objected. "Holidays are as important as school days," he would tell us. "I don't mind as long as they're at school for sports day." So holidays were taken between the beginning and end of June.

On the first year after returning from Canada, come June Ronald got restless.

"How about a holiday?"

"But can we really afford it?" I quibbled.

"No but we'll have one just the same. Perhaps only four or five days in a Highland hotel, somewhere not far away. You know how the kids don't like travelling too far, get impatient and start squabbling. But even a place twelve miles away would seem extremely different country to them. Distance isn't important. At this time of year also, we ought to get something a little bit cheaper and perhaps easy terms for so many."

And so we landed in a hotel in Loch Rannoch. I shall never forget that first holiday after our hard years abroad when holidays had not even been a consideration. It was only for four days but it seemed a lot longer. The place was so different even although it was no more than fifty miles from home – a rambling low-ceilinged country hotel with its mixture of grandeur and simplicity. The broad stairs ran down to the large red carpeted hall at the bottom of which stood an enormous Chinese bowl, beautifully-patterned in blues, reds, golds, used for holding every kind of walking stick you can imagine. The large dining room boasted white-clothed tables, gleaming cutlery and glasses.

There was a scattering of older people staying at the hotel – mostly couples. One couple, rather younger than the others, every mealtime tried to put on the style – always immaculately and correctly dressed and speaking in loud posh accents, they had obviously been the centre of attraction – the focal point of the dining room. However when we came along this was no longer the case. They were shifted to the side and two tables were put together for us in the centre. I could not help enjoying this to a degree. I was proud of my children.

There were five of them then. Richard was the oldest at seven and though rather unruly at home they were well-behaved when out, an attractive bunch I thought, and I had them dressed in inexpensive but neat shorts and tee-shirts and jerseys of my own knitting. I felt a sense of achievement that other people, older people should enjoy our children and Ronald and I were pleased when we got praise for them.

Outside was sheer delight – the mountains, the loch, the narrow winding road with sheep wandering everywhere unwilling to move for the passing car. Inside and out there was the faint smell of woodsmoke. When it was sunny a long lane of sun-diamonds danced off the loch. When the rain came it was gentle – the wind was soft and all the faint smells of woods and wild flowers would subtly permeate the air. Ronald hired a boat and took the boys fishing. I was left with the two wee ones Mahri-Louise and Grant. I had time to play with them or walk for a short way up the quiet Highland road and snatch a conversation with another holidaymaker – no housework to do and no meals to prepare. For several years this was the sort of holiday we took.

Some time after Kathleen was born, one fine day Ronald said, "I think we should do something a little different this year for our holidays. Rent a house somewhere in the Highlands for a fortnight." We got hold of the *Courier*, and looked down the column for holiday houses to let and came up with Clunes Lodge. Or rather Ronald did. I thought it too big and grand but it cost only £17 a week.

"Could be fun," said Ronald, "and you know the Robertsons

who have come to live in the cottage down the road. They've just retired and have come back to live in Perthshire where they belong after living most of their lives in London. Jim Robertson was a butler there and his wife was the cook to some Lord or other. I was talking to them the other day and they told me that every summer they used to come up to Scotalnd and work at a shooting lodge. I'll ask them if they would come with us. I'd pay them of course."

Ronald and the children loved that first year at Clunes. The space and the freedom of it for the children; and Ronald, from time to time, had a tendency to like grandeur and to imagine he was some duke. And you could at Clunes with its solidly furnished bedrooms, innumerable bathrooms, broad staircase, wide hall and long dining room. At mealtimes Ronald would sit at the top of the long table and preside over his children – with pictures of stags and Highland game all round us, a huge log fire sparking in the hearth and the delicious meals that Mrs Robertson had prepared for us. Her husband kept the whole place warm by stoking the boiler.

I did have reservations about Clunes. In spite of the Robertsons' contribution it was a lot of work for me and a worry over the safety of the children. The road that is now the A9 ran between the lodge and the River Garry and although the road had very little traffic compared with what it has today, it was still dangerous. At the bottom of the sward of green wilderness that lay between the lodge and the road was a three-feet high stone dyke. The retired gamekeeper's wife who lived nearby sympathised with me.

"I've seen the children," she said in her soft Highland lilt. "You just can't stop them. They're over the wall like weasels." The River Garry was also a cause for some concern. It wasn't exactly a safe river especially when it was in spate. The boys were always determined to go fishing and Michael, an especially dedicated fisher, used to stay away for hours and hours coming back with enough trout for us all for breakfast. There was a swing bridge over the river opposite the lodge which also left a lot to be desired from the safety angle. It stood high above the river and had many of its boards rotten or missing altogether. However, that year we did all get home safely and everyone wanted to go again the following year.

By then the Robertsons had moved on and we took Jane with us. We had quite a number of visitors that year. My mother and father, my sister and family. My sister was now married with two little children much the same age as Lindsay and Kathleen. A friend also came to stay for a few days with his four young daughters. He had been recently widowed and left with the young girls. He made a most loving and caring father. The children did have fun. I remember that year especially, transferring tadpoles from the river into a huge wooden tub of water.

I sometimes went with Ronald to the pub in the evenings. It was a couthy place where an alarm clock went off at 11pm to let everyone know it was closing time and then the party began! When Ronald went there for the first time several gamekeepers had beaten him to it.

"Give the lads a beer," said Ronald to the publican.

"They'll tak a nip," was his response.

Another time when Ronald noticed a tadpole swimming in his glass of whisky, he showed it to the publican and was told, "Ach the Garry always does that when it's in spate." Whereupon the publican curled his finger inside the glass and removed the offending creature.

His wife had been, what she termed, "on the boards" – could dance, sing, entertain and sometimes gave us a concert of her own making. All in all, it was always an enjoyable night. I loved also, all the outside things – the birds and butterflies, even the snakes. I never saw any snakes on our first visit but this year there were quite a few, or was it that Jane was just good at finding them.

Jane had happened to hear there were adders around and had made a great fuss. "Are they poisonous?" she asked. "I'm terrified of snakes."

"There are adders and they are poisonous to certain people but don't fuss Jane, I never saw one last year." Jane found half a dozen. I think she went looking for them and then one day, she shrieked, "Mrs Gillies, Mrs Gillies – a snake – a great big one!"

So we all trooped out to look and there it lay on the greenest of moss – a real beauty with wonderful gold and black markings down its back. It had just changed skin and the old skin lay at its side. It didn't move, just lay there enjoying the sun. Alan, Jean's husband, ran for his camera but the minute he came back with it the snake slipped down a crack in the ground and was gone.

For all the good sides of Clunes I was glad just the same when it was not available for rent the next year. It had been fun but a lot of work also. Next year we found another place from the *Courier*. Further away this time in the West Highlands on the Morvern peninsula.

"Further to go but only three bedrooms, Margaret." This place suited us to perfection. It was quite a bit off the beaten track with single track roads with passing places leading to the village of Lochaline. Not long after we arrived someone said to us, "Oh so you've come back to visit your old home have you?" We didn't know what he was talking about. We asked him what he meant.

"Your name is Gillies, isn't it? Well you'll find a lot of the people here are also called Gillies – Gillies or Laurie. That is because they are the people who are left of those evacuated from St Kilda in the 1930s." The man explained that the people were brought to what was thought to be one of the quietest and most remote parts of Scotland so that they would feel more at home. Many of them, unfortunately died of tuberculosis. "Your house, Larachbeg, I think I am right in saying, was built for them. Certainly they lived in it."

We all loved Lochaline. Ronald took the boys fishing in the forgotten hill lochs, while I lay in the sun in the wild grassy garden that someone had once loved with its diverted burn, old apple tree, irises and rhododendrons. Overhead flew innumerable huge dragonflies with gold and black striped bodies, for all the world like small helicopters. There were plenty of birds and butterflies for me to watch, always a hobby of mine, and there were walks round the loch to the ruined castle of the Lord of the Isles. Half way along there was an abundance of fossils. Down on the beach too there were all sorts of rock pools for the children to watch and study. When you first approached them all was still but if you sat quietly for a while all sorts of shells and things began to move.

We'd break off a stem of sea thrift and tickle the ruby red sea anemones into spreading out their numerous arms which fooled them into thinking the tide was coming in with more food. The children were fascinated and spent hours on the rocks. At lunchtime we would sometimes have a bite to eat in the one and only hotel – always an excitement for children – eating out with sometimes an impromptu concert thrown in, given by the local lads playing fiddle, accordian and mouth organ.

My definition of a good holiday was to get everyone back in one piece. The children in their wild excitement at being in a new place always seemed to want to throw themselves off a mountain or into a ravine or find a boat with a hole in it that would sink. But in spite of everything I enjoyed these holidays.

Chapter 11
Trouble Comes in Threes

When the children were all young, like mothers everywhere, my own forms of recreation were pretty thin on the ground. I read about people who didn't think they were fully stretched. That was never my complaint. I always felt fully stretched with little ones at home. They seemed to sense the moment you weren't thinking about them and act accordingly so I didn't even read much until after Kathleen went to school. But I did have some simple things that gave me a lot of pleasure.

"I've got a surprise for you," said Ronald to me one day not long before Lindsay was born. "It'll maybe arrive when I'm down the fields ploughing. That's why I'm telling you. Don't send it back. It's for you."

And come the surprise did in a big white van. I could hardly believe my eyes when the driver pulled out an expensive-looking pedigree pram. It was a beautiful shape – cream inside, black outside with a white flower pattern in the centre – a roomy pram with large wheels. I had mentioned to Ronald I would need some kind of a pram but never expected this aristocrat. For the first three boys I had an old pram lent to me by my sister-in-law and for the Canada babies a small buggy type needed for travelling, but this was beautiful.

"It's lovely Ronald," I said when he came back home giving him a hug. "What a surprise, but can we afford it?"

"If I can borrow for a new tractor I can borrow for a pram," he said. After Lindsay was born, whenever I could manage it, I was off wheeling the pram the two miles to Errol showing off my gorgeous new baby. The roads were quiet in those days and at certain times of the year the countryside was beautiful with fields a brilliant emerald or rustling cloth of gold.

Errol was a typical Scottish village. It was built on one of the few bits of high ground, or Inches, as they are called, that rose out of what had once been marshland. A hill ran up to the village passing the garage, the school, a mansion house in its policy of trees, and three other substantial houses in which lived the banker, the doctor and the headmaster. To the right lay the church which I always thought was a handsome edifice, although some people told me the architecture was all wrong – "too many different styles all welded together". I liked it, especially its tall square tower that could be seen for miles, at the top of which was a clock that rang out the hours in mellow tones. Sometimes when the air was still at midnight we could hear it down at the farm two miles away. Further to the right stretched the large tree-lined park with its view towards the hills. It could be cold there when a wind was blowing. On the day of the annual school sports there was often a wind blowing.

The narrow road to the village rounded a bend at the small post office and continued on up past plain two-storey houses and shops built of stone, brick or clay, many of which were covered in harling in different shades of grey or beige. The pavements were narrow and there were no gardens at the fronts.

Near the top of the village was the cross marked by a unicorn. A little further on at the big wrought iron gates of Errol Park Estate, the road divided into two, one fork running north to the brickworks, the other south following the course of the river.

We were lucky in Errol. There was still a variety of shops – two butchers, two grocers, a baker, a draper that sold an enormous range of goods, a post office, a hairdresser, a chip shop and two pubs. We also had a dispensing doctor – everything we needed in fact. Even today Errol hasn't changed much but there is no baker or draper any more, the mansion at the foot of the village with its grounds has gone to make way for a housing development and the banker, doctor and headmasker no longer inhabit the same large houses in the village that they once did.

The pram proved to be most useful as well as a pleasure. Because of its large wheels it was possible to push it round the rough farm road and because of its large size I used it when one of the small children was ill as a bed in the kitchen which saved me going up and down stairs. It's still in use now with the eleventh grandchild.

I had always liked walking and seeing the wild birds, animals and flowers so whenever there was the slightest opportunity I would go for a walk round the farm – sometimes very early in the morning and before anyone was up, sometimes even in the middle of the night under the moon and stars when the owl would smooth out of the barn on woollen wings giving me a fright as I passed.

I used time to the best possible advantage. Sometimes I was so exhausted by the time I'd got all the children to bed that I went to bed myself with a lot of the housework undone and then I would get up about two in the morning to do two hours hard work. What a lot I could get done with no one about, no phone or door bell ringing. I'd go back to bed and when I got up a few hours later tell myself the fairies had been in and done all the work while I was asleep.

One day a friend of mine in Perth was telling me about the keep fit class she had just joined.

"You must come," she said. "It's fun. You could do with at least one night out a week." Ronald thought it a good idea.

"I'll easily look after the kids," he said, so I joined. In a short while I had a few going with me from the Errol district. We took turn about driving and it was fun. Led by a rather beautiful amazon of a girl with a good sense of humour everyone enjoyed it. There would be about a hundred of us mostly from Perth. The pianist was good and the tunes lively. Afterwards I and my friends from Errol went for brown bread, cucumber sandwiches and coffee before going home. Ronald, teasing me, called it the keep fat club saying that it consolidated what I'd got but agreed it had made a difference to my life.

Perhaps I enjoyed the company of the others as much as anything, the chat, the exchange of news. Perhaps with having the biggest family I always seemed to have the most traumatic happenings in the week.

"Well what happened this week?" they would ask as soon as we got out on to the main road. There would always be something to report.

"Do you remember me telling you a fortnight ago that Richard had the chickenpox. Well the other six have it now. I wasn't going to come tonight but Ronald insisted. They are not all that ill, just fractious and what a problem I have trying to keep the little ones from scratching their spots." One of my friends came along next day and spent time helping me with the children.

By the time Kathleen was two Lindsay went to school. I had now only one at home for the first time for sixteen years. And then devastation struck. It's odd how things often come in threes both disasters and triumphs. As far as I was concerned the next few years became the time of disasters.

First my beloved mother took a severe stroke. She was approaching eighty and had had one or two minor ones in previous years but she had always seemed so young and full of life, always unconcerned about herself and optimistic for my sister's and my future. My father called me over one evening in alarm when she took ill. When I arrived I found her in a state of high excitement.

"I think this is it," she said, "but you're not to worry. I've had a good life and I don't mind at all."

After she had said these words the doctor arrived and she was bundled off to hospital. These were the last coherent words I heard my mother say although she was to live another four years. My sister now living in Edinburgh with her husband and two pre-school age children was as stunned as I was. For several days mother's life hung in the balance and then after a brain operation which relieved the pressure, they believed she would live but with much incapacity. My sister came to be with her whenever she could in the first week. Then things settled down a little and I kept Jean informed of mother's progress over the phone. Worse devastation was to come.

One evening about a couple of weeks after my mother took her stroke, I phoned my sister to give her the latest report. She sounded more cheerful over the phone. She'd bought a carpet that day for the spare room in the new house they had just bought and she was painting the doors. She had a bit of a sore throat but she expected it would pass off – nothing much.

At six o'clock next morning the phone woke me at my

bedside. In the darkness I picked it up in alarm. Who would phone at this time in the morning – the hospital? It was Jean's husband Alan at the other end of the phone.

"Jean's dead," he sobbed. I found it extremely hard to take this message in. I just couldn't believe it. Although I had seen death often enough during my years of training as a nurse this was the first time I had lost anyone close. I found Alan's message impossible to take in – beyond tears.

"It's not possible," I said. "I was just speaking to her last night. She seemed more cheerful than since mother's stroke."

"She got up in the night to go to the bathroom and that's where I found her on the floor, dead."

I could hear he was having difficulty in speaking.

"We'll be right over." I put down the phone.

I won't linger on the next few dreadful days – the devastated husband – the poor little children. They say there are many indispensable people buried in graveyards. But perhaps the most indispensable person of all is a mother. A real mother cannot be replaced. The post mortem revealed that my sister had died of the current flu virus that was on the rampage that year killing young people. The verdict was that the virus had gone straight to the heart muscle, paralysing it.

After the funeral another tremendous task remained to be done. My mother had to be told.

"Does she really need to know?" I asked the doctor, tears in my eyes.

"Yes she does," said the most sympathetic lady doctor. "She really does. Your mother may live for quite a while and she'll wonder what's happened. I know your mother cannot speak and we are not sure how much she understands but it might be more than we think. She must be told."

"But how can I ever do it and I know Dad won't be able to. He can hardly talk about it to me. He's never been good with words."

"I'll do it," said the doctor. "I'll do it. It really would be best coming from me. We're not sure what reaction she might have and I'll need to be there."

And so my mother was told. How much she understood

we'll never know because, apart from the odd word, she never regained her speech. But we know she understood and when from time to time we saw the silent tears cruising down her cheeks, we knew she was thinking of the daughter she had lost and knew there was no real comfort for the loss of a daughter.

My father wasn't an overtly emotional man. It was difficult for him to express feelings and I being rather like him understood. He needed my company a lot during this period which was sometimes difficult with all my other commitments. He also had not been well – had been bothered off and on with a bleeding ulcer – was waiting to go into hospital for an operation. The appointment came up about a fortnight after Jean's funeral.

"You'll have to go," said the doctor. "We don't want you bleeding to death." Dad didn't seem to care one way or the other. Life seemed finished for him anyway.

"Probably won't come out of hospital," he said to me the day before he went in.

"Of course you will," I said, "and Dad, Ronald and I have had an idea. One of the cottages is empty just now. How would you like to come and live with us? You would be on your own but close to us. You can't go on living in that rambling house any longer especially if you need a while to recuperate. It's too far from the shops or the chemist for a start and it would make life easier for me not having to run over to Newport all the time." This last argument settled it.

"Well, if I come out of hospital, that might be a good idea. We've all got to stand together now, those who are left of us," he said. He agreed to us clearing out his house while he was in hospital, taking the decisions as to what needed to be sold. Ronald was a tower of strength to me over this period. He got the men from the farm over and we all set to. Disposing of a lifetime's goods and chattels is never easy but perhaps it was easier for us than it would have been for Dad.

We had said, "Now Dad, tell us what you particularly want to keep," and this had been done. It was at this time that I came across, tucked away in the corner of the attic, a green shoebox stuffed full of every one of the airmail letters I had written to my father and mother. She had said, "One day you will write a book about your adventure."

I had never really believed her but rather liked the idea.

And so Dad came to stay with us in the small cottage we had made comfortable for him. Some arrangements had been made also with Alan and the children. His work was in Edinburgh and he would have to stay there. Somehow he would manage to look after the children in term time – Catriona had just gone to school – Kenny could go to nursery school.

"If you can manage in term time I'll take them during the holidays," I said.

And so it was arranged. They came to the farm for most of their holidays in the years before Catriona was old enough to be on her own. What were two more children, I thought. But I used to think it really would have been easier to have had them all the time. They would have fitted in with the others more easily. Sometimes there seemed to be tension especially when they first arrived. They were brought up so differently – not accustomed to the rough and tumble and inclined to brood. But then they were not mine and I knew it was all that Alan had left. He needed them. He was their father doing his best to work and look after them at the same time.

"Did you like coming down to the farm?" I asked Catriona at a much later date when she was a young lady with a university degree. "Did you find it difficult? Our life must have been so different to yours in Edinburgh and your cousins could be a bit rough at times."

"Oh no we loved it," she said, "looked forward to it greatly – couldn't wait."

With my dad settled into the cottage and arrangements made for the motherless children there still remained the problem of my mother. The doctors took some time to assess her and her future requirements but they finally decided she would need to go into a nursing home and asked us which we would prefer – Perth or Dundee – we said Perth and as luck would have it there was a free bed in one of Perth's nicest nursing homes.

However I wasn't too happy about this – mother in a nursing home however nice. How would her independent spirit take to this? Perhaps I could take her – get help. I went to Doctor Edington with my proposal.

"Now look here," he said emphatically. "Your mother has been lucky enough to get into one of Perth's best nursing homes. I couldn't have arranged that. You won't get the chance again. And," he said, making the ultimate argument that he knew would get to me, "it wouldn't be fair to your mother. With the best help in the world you couldn't look after her as well as they would in hospital."

As if all that wasn't enough, out of the blue, Ronald had a slight heart attack. All the tests were done.

"Rather unusual case," Dr Edington told me. "He's had this problem for a long time. Perhaps he had rheumatic fever or something when he was young. His heart should have enlarged a bit to compensate but for some reason it hasn't."

This explained the difficulty Ronald had experienced with long sustained hard work. His father had liked to call it laziness which it hadn't been. Also he was having trouble with his legs due to certain hardening of the arteries. His nerves were bad.

"People talk about nerves," he said. "Nerves! Ever since I was young I've been able to feel every nerve in my body."

The doctor wanted him to go into hospital for what might be quite a lengthy stay.

"I can't," he said to me, "I can't leave you and the children. How could you manage to run a farm and look after all the kids. You don't even have help just now."

This was true as Jane had been gone a couple of years and Mrs Hodge who was once my mainstay now worked at a neighbouring farmer's hens.

"I'll get someone if I get stuck," I assured Ronald, "and I'll give you a daily bulletin of what's happening on the farm and we've always got Dave Scott the grieve. He'll know what needs to be done. He'll keep me right."

Ronald reluctantly agreed. The doctors warned me he would need to stay for the complete treatment but I knew Ronald would refuse to do that if things were going wrong on the farm. So they just had to go right. Mostly we didn't have too many animals, just cattle or lambs to fatten in the autumn. But this year we had some in-calf heifers. He'd bought them at a neighbour's sale. They'd been a bargain. Most of them had calved well. I would only have one or two to worry about. On the last day of March the remaining heifer started to calf.

Dave Scott came in about teatime a bit worried about her.

"Come and have a look," he said, "she's been at it a wee while."

I went over to the byre. She was sitting down looking rather uncomfortable. Remembering my own births I said, "Oh she'll probably be all right. It can take some time. No two are alike."

Dave and I kept a watchful eye on her all that evening. I went to the byre just before midnight fully expecting to see a calf – nothing. The heifer was standing up and I saw two small hooves of her calf. Trouble – the calf was coming the wrong way. I would have to get help but who? I had been so well trained not to think of vets unless as a last resort. Vets were expensive – could take away any profit there was on an animal. Dave Scott didn't know about animals. He was an arable man. And then I thought of our nearest neighbour. Jim had a dairy and knew all about calfing cows – that was his life.

It was five minutes past midnight when I phoned. A sleepy voice answered.

"A cow calving at Inchmichael – what time is it?"

I thought this an odd question but obligingly looked at the clock. "A minute past midnight."

"By that's a clever one," he said, "you're quick off your mark. I wonder who put you up to it. But I'm not so easily April fooled."

It took me a wee while to get through to him that this was no April fool, this was for real. But when I did he was over at Inchmichael in no time at all and the heifer safely delivered. He had brought with him his new equipment that he had acquired at the Smithfield Show in the winter. I admired his expertise, his instant handling of the situation as good as any vet's, his bravery. Heifers especially can be a bit obstreperous in these situations.

"No trouble – any time," he said and was gone, back for a short rest no doubt, before he got up at 3am for the milking.

I was able to tell Ronald next day that all the heifers were safely delivered. That could have been an instance of losing both cow and calf.

The Spring wore on. I hadn't realised until now how difficult farming really was – the decisions that had to be made taking into account what the weather might do.

We had only two men and they had a lot to do getting land ready for the sowing of peas, spring barley etc. As the crops grew you had to watch there was nothing going wrong. The number of things that could happen to them was incredible. I took to walking round the fields whenever I could get the chance and taking wee Kathleen with me. She was a great wee walker and the only one at home now. Walking round the fields was not exactly a chore that Spring. The weather was comparatively good and the crops took on that unbelievable emerald – the straight blades of wheat, the curly barley. Curlew, lapwings, oyster catchers came back to nest in the growing fields, larks were everywhere singing. In May all along the pow where the water hens nested, the hawthorn bloomed thicker than ever. On the long verges of the farm road, Lady Ann's Lace was a white flourish that swayed in the wind. I worked out my itinerary for the day on these walks. The afternoons were most likely spent in hospital visiting. Kathleen came with me. She was my little comfort in everything. I realised it was good for children to see the unwell and disabled from an early age. Young children take everything in naturally and how much patients in hospital liked to see a bright little girl!

Hay time came. The weather was threatening to break down. Would we be able to get it all in in time. The weather kept up long enough – only one field to go but quite a big one – the bales of hay all lay scattered about – and had to be gathered up. It was in the days when the bales were small square ones.

I remembered what Ronald would have done. He would have got any spare man to help from the village, out of the pub. It was the weekend. I asked Dave Scott – would he do it? Rather to my surprise he refused. "It'll be okay. The weather'll hold," he said.

I didn't think it would. I went to the village myself and looked into that very much male domain.

"Any volunteers to bring in the hay," I shouted through the

beer-smelling, smoky air. I got several. We got the hay in and the heavens opened.

"Hay's in safely," I was able to report to Ronald next day rather to his surprise.

The main ordeal was to come, however – the dreaded pea crop.

"Worst tempered crop on the farm," Ronald would say and he was right. But until I was in the situation myself I hadn't quite understood what he meant. Peas in those days were cut in the fields and then brought in in great green loadfuls to the static viners. These viners were often shared by one or two farmers. We shared ours with our nearest neighbour. The harvesting of peas more than any other crop was at the mercy of the weather. July with its wet warm days could bring them on quickly or if it was cooler and dry they would take some time to ripen. It was impossible to foretell what it would be. This year the sun shone warmly, interspersed with short showers. The peas ripened quickly and were a good crop. The trouble with peas was that in one afternoon of sun they could over ripen become too hard and the factory wouldn't take them – they had to be dumped. This year, to begin with the pea harvest went well enough but because of the sun and warm weather they were all ripening at once. Our neighbour was in the same boat. Tensions were running high. One field was threatening to be overripe.

"We'll have to get those cut and in the viner today," I said to Dave Scott.

"It's not our turn," I was told.

And it wasn't. I asked our neighbour but his were on the brink also. What could I do? It was his turn. We lost that field of peas.

Still half the crop to harvest. I wasn't managing too well. I shouldn't have told Ronald of the loss but we were so used to telling the truth to one another.

He signed himself out of hospital next day. As with many farmers the farm was more important than his health.

Mixed Feelings of a Farmer's Wife

The burns ran full
While the river rose,
The sky stayed a sober, sombre grey,
Tall trees hunched
Over field floods
And cars on the road threw clouds of spray.

Dull hills hid
Behind screens of rain,
Bedraggled birds left the watered air.
For two dreich days
And two dour nights
Wet dripping sounds were everywhere.

The third day's sun
Shone from deep blue,
I saw with joy through my window pane
A bright new loch
Where white swans sailed
But would waterlogged wheat grow again?

Chapter 12
Empty Nest

With Ronald restored to comparative health things settled down into a more usual routine. Kathleen went to school. My small companion wasn't around so much. In a way I was desolate. This was the first time I hadn't had a child around my feet for nineteen years. I knew I must have no more. It wasn't fair to Ronald. Also my first born, Richard, had left home.

Influenced by the stories Ronald had told them about his time in the navy during the war – the places he had seen and what a big and interesting world it was out there – joining the navy became Richard's ambition. Like his father before him he had a certain degree of colour blindness which gave him two choices should he join – a cook or communicator. Like his father he chose the latter.

Richard hoped to see the world. Although we hadn't been able to take them about much, other than places in Scotland, all the children seemed to have this desire to see the world. Perhaps it was the map of the world always up on the yellow kitchen wall beside the gallery of their own works of art that had something to do with it. They had a game that they played a lot. See who can find . . .

I didn't realise at the time that when they flew the nest, they would try to find some of these outlandish places they had first discovered on the map. After a year at *HMS Mercury* near Peterborough, from which he had passed out with flying colours, Richard went to sea. Now I would never be sure where he was and the cod wars were looming up.

I still had more than plenty to do. I took over most of the driving and helped Ronald wherever I could but with my babies all growing up I felt an unexplainable void – a vacuum needing to be filled.

One day while cleaning out some drawers long left unattended, I came across an old jotter I had bought in Canada. I remembered it was in this that I had written the poems when we had first arrived in Canada and were completely isolated on the farm on the Prairie – no phone, no radio, no transport, no one to speak to. Should I open the jotter and read them? Should I stick it in the Aga along with the other rubbish? They would probably be awful – make me cringe. Curiosity got the better of me and sitting down on the spare bedroom carpet on a warm patch of sunlight coming in from the bay window I tentatively opened the book.

It was like looking through an old photograph album you had forgotten about. The poems brought back to me vividly what I had seen and felt in those lonely days in Canada. I remembered the urge within me to describe this fantastic new world I had been catapulted into. And I remembered more than that. I remembered my mother saying after listening to a childish verse I had made up, "One day you'll be a poet, Margaret."

I'd liked the idea of that. My mother had been a great lover of poetry and I had been brought up on a diet of Byron and Burns, Wordsworth and Tennyson. She could recite screeds of their work. I loved the sounds of the words. I wrote away when I was young – poetry, small plays, letters to people – and when fifteen had won a competition on the radio in Aunt Kathleen's Children's Hour.

An aunt hearing the programme was derogatory about the poem I had written – 'nice little pen picture'. That was of course all that it was, but her words and the tone they were delivered in had the effect of putting me right off writing poetry. I was growing up into the real world. Who was I to think I could be a poet? I gave up the idea altogether. A couple of years later when wondering what I was going to do with my life I did try to get into journalism. Through the golf course, my father knew the editor of the *Sunday Post*.

"Tell her to send me some of her work," was the offer.

I did so and went for an interview. He was complimentary about my writing but criticised my spelling and asked me questions about day-to-day events, the names of footballers, who was Marilyn Monroe? etc. I knew none of the answers.

"Go home, learn to spell better, read the current news every day and come back to me in a year," was the verdict.

But I never did – life took over. I fell in love for the first time, and my mother nearly died of pneumonia and had to give up teaching. I wanted to do something practical with my life – help people in need. The new national health service was crying out for nurses and with no qualifications of any kind, I was taken on. Looking back I think they must have been pretty desperate. Ever since then I hadn't had an idle moment and here I was, for a short space of time, the dreamer again.

Another two small events happened about the same time as finding the jotter. I read somewhere a statement that got to me. "If there is something you have always wanted to do why not try it now. If you're no good, it won't matter but if you never try you will never know." In another paper I saw an advert for a poetry competition in a writers' magazine. I sent away for it. I was fascinated. There seemed to be a world going on that I knew nothing about. One of the articles was written by a poet, Margaret Munro Gibson. She talked of an underworld of poetry very much alive within subscription magazines – write her if you want more information. I did just that. She was most helpful and eventually I sent her some poems. She was most encouraging – gave constructive criticism and told me to start sending one or two to magazines. She wouldn't let me stop until I got the first one published which was a day of joy for me. I had kept my new occupation completely secret getting up at five in the morning to write but with the first one published I dared tentatively to tell Ronald. He seemed pleased and encouraged me to continue.

Why not join a creative writing class? I had seen one advertised at the Perth Tech – once a week in the evenings. A new world was opening up for me.

Chapter 13

The Spice of Life

There were about fifteen of us at the creative writing class that year. For two sessions – Autumn and Spring it cost us £8 – not too difficult to afford. The man who ran it, Mr Douglas, taught us a lot. If we had any complaint it was that the class was rather geared towards writing in Scots and around a folk culture. Some of us had a wider field in mind. Perhaps what I enjoyed most was the companionship of like minds where so many things were up for discussion. Here, for a short while, I could forget all the things that seemed to be going wrong in my life. Plus it gave me directions and incentives about what to write.

I would stick to poetry. Poetry was my first love and poems need not be long. In my busy days I had no time to write anything long. A year or two earlier I had been invited to a party in a caravan. Jean MacCormack is of the family now big in caravans and Jean herself was to become Perth's Lady Provost for a number of years. At the party Jean had a fortune teller – a well-known Dundee lady. I'm not given to fortune telling and I was told a lot of things that never happened but the main thing she said when she looked at my hand was, "You have things to say. Start now, go out and say them." I thought about this from time to time – but how? Now I knew.

Most of the poems were composed while walking round the fields in all weathers in solitude which I did whenever I could escape – a line would come into my head and that would be it started.

At the end of that year's class several of us were very much looking forward to meeting up the following session but the fees shot up to £15 and some were dissatisfied because of the emphasis on Scottish writing. Fewer than eight registered and the class was cancelled. A few of us were unhappy about this and decided to do something about it.

"Let's set up a writing club of our own – find a hotel room somewhere. If we got enough people to come we need not charge more than £8 a year."

That is exactly what we did. We got a room in the Lovat House Hotel in Perth at a reasonable rate and put an advert in the local paper. Twenty five people enrolled. We were in business. From our wee group or steering committee as it would be grandly called today, we had chosen Jean Munro as president. She was a farmer's wife and with a great deal of experience in running various types of groups. With her help a really good constitution was agreed upon which stood us in good stead to this day, namely the president would be president for one year only when the vice president would automatically take over, secretaries and treasurers for two years only, then a compulsory year off committee altogether. This I see now probably kept any one clique from taking over and eventually killing the enterprise.

One of the first things we did as a group was to become affiliated to the Scottish Association of Writers, a body that was growing in membership all the time. Once a year they held a conference in a Pitlochry hotel. These were exceedingly good containing a vast amount of competitions often adjudicated by top writers from all over Britain. We ourselves, in our own group, were able to get many well-known and interesting speakers. Over the years we had many famous Scots. Ian Crichton Smith, Nigel Tranter, Norman McCaig, Tessa Ransford, Duncan Glen and many more well-known figures in the Scottish writing scene.

A year later another group sprang up, this time in Dundee. The atmosphere in our meeting place, a small library, was right for this little group. It was very different from the bigger group but it did turn out to be the one I did most work for. It met fortnightly as did the Perth group but we had no speakers, no competitions and instead four or five words were set to see if we could come up with anything. This was always a challenge and it was amazing sometimes what was produced. I found it a great catalyst giving me a much wider field to write in. The evenings were taken up reading out what we had written and discussion of the work produced. As a rule all of us wrote something completely different using the same starting words.

At the same time I was progressing with my underworld of poetry magazines. Margaret Munro Gibson had advised me on some of the best ones to get – *Poetry Nottingham, Envoi, Outposts* and I was beginning to get more and more of my poems published. Margaret warned me, "*Outposts*," she wrote, "is the most difficult one to get into. Howard Sergeant, the editor, has a great reputation – he's started off some now famous poets. His magazine is the longest running, largely self-funding magazine. It won't be easy to get in there but you can try. Most of the poems he uses are in free verse."

> "poems need not be long – in my busy days I had no time to write anything long"

"Try free verse," she wrote, "send them to me and I'll tell you honestly what I think."

This was the release I needed – the poems came. This was the medium I could work best in. I'd never really considered it before having been brought up largely with poems that were more formal. I sent some of my first free verse poems to the editor, Howard Sergeant. He didn't accept any of these first poems for his magazine but wrote saying he felt that since I had reached a certain level in my poetry, would I consider publishing a collection. He offered to do it. I couldn't quite take in what I read and even then I didn't realise what an honour it was to be taken on by Howard. He got so many poets asking him, both here and in the States, to publish collections for them and he refused.

I wrote back agreeing to his suggestion.

"Send me about forty or so and I'll probably choose about twenty-five for a first collection."

But I hadn't got forty. I hastily began to write more hoping they would be good enough. I sent them off in trepidation. The answer came back – he would publish twenty-eight of them. And so my first book, *Give Me the Hill-Run Boys* was born.

Howard did three collections for me before he sadly died. He was a great help. The letters he sent were always short and often contained a rebuke for something wrong I had done and this way I learned. But he was a truly great man and did so very much for his poets. He really cared about the poetry, made, I suspect very little from it financially. He had a daytime job as an accountant and had many hard knocks in the poetry world. He was an excellent poet himself but left very little time for his own writing. I remember once saying in a letter how wonderful the world of poetry was and how kind and helpful poets were. He wrote back and said, "You do not know the half of it. There are no depths to which some poets will not go to get their work into print." He did not agree with me at all.

At a later date Donald Campbell, the Scottish playwright said, "You think it's good at the top. Well I can tell you it's not. It's hell at the top."

So poetry and writing in general wasn't all roses. But I had much more modest aims in mind. To be published was enough. I didn't want to enter into a nasty arena.

Legend

*Centuries ago a French trading ship was wrecked
on the treacherous rocks off the east Aberdeenshire coast. Miraculously, the captain's twin baby
sons were saved, along with the ship's log. The
boys were brought up by local fisher folk and
married into the community.*

My mother lived a legend.
Dark-haired vivacious,
Vivid as November's morning star,
She claimed to be a hark-back
To the French – (the other half of that 'Auld Alliance')
To one of the twins snatched form the roaring seas.
She did much to make this myth come true:
Brought foreign thought to young parochial minds,
Inspired us with French stories.

Her imagination lit our lives.

Once we saw her weep –
The day France fell
And for a while
Light vanished from the courtyard,
Yet after the first strong shock
Her faith returned –
"One day!" she said, "One day . . ."

from *Looking Towards Light*

Chapter 14
Mother and Father

My mother died after being four years in the nursing home. She was eighty-two. In these four years she never regained the use of her limbs nor her speech but she could understand well enough when we spoke to her. She enjoyed our visits. Often when we were in visiting, Dad would read her a chapter or two from books that he knew she liked.

Looking back it always seemed to be sunny in that room with the big bay window overlooking the river and Perth. Always the swifts seemed to be screaming overhead in the summer air but there must have been grey days. There were three other patients in the room mother was in. All variously incapacitated. The one I remember most was Sheila Duffy. She became a special friend of mother's, used to speak for her when we came to visit and loved to listen to the stories my father read out. Sheila was half my mother's age and incapacitated from the neck down but her mind was as agile and alert as a young girl. She was a true romantic and loved nothing better than to relate to us stories of her youth on the west coast of Ireland – the house with the turf roof she was brought up in and the peat she gathered for the winter fire.

Hillside Home was a nice place to be. The nurses were kind – couldn't do enough for their patients – and the food was good. But there was a lack of outside company. Not many people came to visit so visitors were shared and clung onto. The patients never wanted us to go, desperate to know, be a part of outside life. The novice priests from the monastery up on the hill used to visit the patients. They were young and always full of good cheer. Sometimes they would dress up and put on a play.

Losing mother made a huge gap in our lives especially mine. Perhaps it isn't until your mother's no longer there that you realise just how much you owe her. I owed mine a very great deal. She and my father had given me a happy childhood and I don't know anything better than that to get people off to a good start.

She had had a tough life herself. Brought up on a small Aberdeenshire farm, one of seven children, with money often in short supply, they had to fight to get what they wanted. Mother wanted to go to university. It would not be easy. In order to get a better school she was prepared to bike fifteen miles a day. But she probably got a place in the university largely because so many of the boys had gone off to the Great War. She got an MA and then a teaching certificate. Jobs were not easily come by for women even after the Great War with so many men killed but barely had she time to get one before she fell for and married a much older man than herself – the factor of the estate where her people had farmed for three hundred years. He died of a heart attack several years after they were married. Mother took over his job as factor, perhaps one of the first lady factors in Scotland. She loved her work – found it varied and interesting but after a while realised that what she wanted more than anything else was a child. In 1928 she met and married my father. I was their first very much wanted child. After my sister was born the depression was in full swing. Dad had to take on a lesser job and salary but at least he had a job and they managed. When the next war came, in order to protect us, mother took us up to the Ochil Hills where she rented a smallholding.

My father, a townsman at heart said of the location, "It's the sort of place you would go to if you'd committed a murder," but agreed to go for our safety.

Here mother cultivated the few acres. This was her war work – providing food for others. It wasn't completely convenient for Dad's job and often he just got home at the weekends. Towards the end of the war, when teachers became scarce, mother got a job in Dundee. She also only got home at the weekends. At fifteen I was considered quite capable of looking after the small holding and my younger sister still at school. It was a lonely life but suited me well enough.

And now she was no longer in this world.

My father was a very different person to my mother. Where

she was vivacious and outgoing, he was reserved and quiet. Where she was erratic and a dreamer he was steady as a rock and content with little as long as he could spend some time playing golf.

When mother died it left a huge gap in my father's life which he hoped, to a certain extent, I would fill. Here lay difficulty. I had so many other commitments. Ronald's health was giving cause for concern. He needed me more and more to do the driving etc. Though growing older, the children all needed me. Fortunately, in his comfortable cottage Dad lived next door to one of the ploughmen and his wife. She was very kind to him, plied him with baking, jam, home-made soup etc. He started going out to golf more often, taking the back roads to Dundee and crossing the river to Tayport to his favourite course, but he needed something more to interest him. He had been talking a lot about the first world war that he had been through in his youth.

"Right through it I was. Joined up as soon as I could. I was in Spillers' London office at the time and my mate and me went down to recruiting barracks and joined up with the London Scottish. They were desperate for young men like us and we were keen to go – couldn't wait to serve king and country, see a bit of the world."

So Dad had once seen the world as exciting. Perhaps he'd got it all knocked out of him in that dreadful war, and was glad of a quiet life. He never talked much about the war to us as children. He never mentioned the horrors, nor the medals he had won. Occasionally he showed us the bullet wounds in his chest.

"Carried, half dead across the desert in a stretcher," he said, "never thought I would see home again." If he did tell us about it it was to praise the stoicism of men and the humour of his Cockney compatriots who often were responsible for keeping up the morale of their fellows.

Dad sang, from time to time, the old war songs – a war which we as children thought must really have been in the dark ages. Otherwise he never talked about it, wanting, I believe, to leave all the horrors of it behind.

But now after mother's death he began to talk of it more and more – not so much the horrors but about the comradeship – that had been great – nothing like it nowadays and especially the time he had served in Salonica.

"What a place that was – desolate country and we didn't ever quite know who we were supposed to be fighting. How I would like to meet up with some of these old comrades again?"

"Well why not, Dad," I said, "I'm sure there's still some of them about. Why not put an ad in the *Courier* and arrange a meeting – a meal or something."

Dad was surprised at the number of replies he got to his advert. He arranged a meal in a hotel in Perth. They all attended. It was a great success and it became an annual event. After three years or so the Provost of Perth, a kindly man, got word of it and gave them a civic reception. The old boys were overwhelmed.

"The forgotten army, that's what we were, the forgotten army." Forgotten no longer, the Provost saw to it that each year after that their annual outing was funded. Dad used to insist that I went with him. At first I tried to wriggle out of it.

"But Dad, I've so much to do." However I went somewhat reluctantly. It would be boring – all these old boys going on about their experiences. But I was wrong. I didn't find it boring in the slightest. It was fascinating. So many characters and so much to say. I learned things I had never dreamed of from them. Some seemed to have instant recall and a vivid way of telling their story – the trenches, the mud, the snakes, the snow, not knowing who the enemy was and the difference in the place today. Some had been back on organised trips. Now it was a green and fertile land. So inspired was I by their experiences that it gave me food for a series of poems.

I often wished Dad would go, while he was still able, on one of these excursions back to Salonica. But he was content with his meetings and with the new interest, friends and comrades he had made.

Not long before he died an archivist came from Manchester to question Dad on his war experiences. Inadvertantly I happened to visit Dad while he was there questioning him.

The man was introduced to me.

"I'm just about finished," he said. "Just a few more questions."

"And in the trenches," he continued, holding the microphone towards my dad. "This comradeship you mention so often was it ever violated? Did any of the soldiers ever let you down?"

"No never," said my father without any hesitation.

"We'll not pursue that line," said the questioner kindly. I heard the disbelief in his voice but perhaps he had come up against this before. Comradeship was immortal. Any wrong doing had been buried with the men – left in the desert, buried in the unconscious – forgotten.

Chapter 15

Richard

Richard remained in the navy for four years. The time he had signed on for, no more. A year was spent at *HMS Mercury* learning his trade. The rest was spent at sea. He did see the world.

We got irregular letters from Richard all of which were interesting and telling us of the wonders he had seen. He didn't dwell on the hardships. Richard was of a hail-fellow-well-met disposition and got on well with the other sailors. He was also of a careful nature. Didn't blow all his money in every port he went into. He told me he became the banker to a few of the other sailors who never learned the art of not spending everything in one mad spree and having nothing until the next pay day.

"You wouldn't believe it, Mum, what some of these lads get up to. Often they're ripped off but they never seem to learn. They end up with nothing until next pay day when they have to pay me back half of what they get. They just don't seem to be able to save anything."

I was glad that Richard wasn't becoming like them. I had always impressed thrift on the children. Perhaps my words were paying off.

As well as regular letters we got unexpected visits. Richard would just arrive. Sometimes it would be in the middle of the night. You never knew when. It was very seldom that he asked us to come and meet him anywhere. Ronald had always taught them to find their own way – look after themselves. Perhaps it was paying off. I would willingly have gone to meet them in Perth, Edinburgh, wherever, to make things easier for them. Ronald would not have encouraged me to do so.

"They must become independent. It'll be better for them in the long run. You'll see." But Richard never asked.

The door on the old farm house was never locked so

occasionally, if he arrived in the middle of the night, I would not hear him creep in. What pure delight to find him there in the morning. Once he arrived just as I was up and dressed – the footsteps outside – the opening of the farm house door – "Richard – how did you get here?"

"Walked from Perth," he said.

"You should have phoned, that must be all of twelve miles."

"Actually, I thoroughly enjoyed the walk. These early summer mornings in the Carse of Gowrie are great. The air is so fresh and everything so vividly green. And you should see the sun coming up over Dundee in the distance."

I knew what he meant. On my early walks I had often seen the same spectacle.

"You don't know what like it is after months and months of wave upon wave to be on dry land again with so much to see. You are inclined to notice every detail. And it's so quiet at that time in the morning. Only one or two lorries passed. It was magic."

Always on Richard's return a crowd gathered to hear of his exploits. He never mentioned anything he thought might worry us in his letters, but when he came home he would tell us, the danger now over.

Fortunately, while Richard was in the navy, there were no major upheavals. The cod wars were the nearest thing to conflict. It was perhaps Richard's most dangerous time at sea.

"Absolutely freezing cold up there off Iceland. Fall in the sea and it would be curtains. I was radio operator for the most part but I had other duties to perform also. The worst one was letting the helicopter off the decks. In freezing winds, in mountainous seas, loosening these planes – had the slightest thing gone wrong, we would have been overboard in a second and that would have been the last of us. I'm not the bravest of people and I can tell you I hand it to these lads that fly these things. Wouldn't have done their job for all the tea in China. They must have nerves of steel. For the most part though it was routine. Mostly it seemed to be a time of waiting to see what would happen. The Russians were there as well waiting in their subs. Got in contact with them sometimes. Unfortunately they couldn't speak much English and we little or no Russian. However in spite of that we managed to get some games going through the radio. You always had to let them win though. Otherwise just the same sort of guys as us. It's the politicians that start the wars not the ordinary people."

Richard was learning.

During a trip round the world we didn't see Richard for a full year. It seemed a long time but there were more stories than ever.

"You should see Sydney – what a great city – one of the biggest harbours I have ever seen. Beautiful. And the buildings – seem to go with the landscape somehow, so tall and all different colours – the streets are like great narrow canyons. There was a thunderstorm while I was there. It was frightening in a way. Great streaks of lightening shooting everywhere and the noise of the thunder resounding in these tremendously deep canyons." Richard went on and on.

"Could have been in a bit of bother there actually," he said a little hesitantly. "Had rather a riotous last night. Don't quite know how I got back on board ship before she sailed. All I remember was being carried aboard by my mates. Got into a bit of trouble over that but nothing to what I would have been in had I missed the ship. That's the greatest crime – not making it."

"Whatever did you . . ." I asked a little hesitantly. I got no further.

"Sowing his wild oats, leave the laddie alone," Ronald said. "What about when you got to America?"

"Got into a spot of bother there too," said Richard ruefully. "Coming back one night along the banks of the Potomac to the ship some of my drunken shipmates pushed me into the river. I suppose I'd had a bit too much as well. It wasn't done with any malice. It was just horseplay and they probably didn't know I couldn't swim. Two or three things saved me I think. Having had a few I didn't panic and the waters of the Potomac are so dirty I don't think you could sink if you tried. I was needing a hair cut. It was getting a bit long. I can't remember quite what happened but seemingly they managed to get hold of my hair and pull me out. After that, on the voyage home, I was really ill. The trouble with the navy is that you can never get them to believe you're not well. I ended up not being able to walk at all, my limbs all seized up. They wouldn't believe me – thought I was putting it on. Eventually they did of course and I went right into hospital when I came back to this country. I was there quite a while but I wasn't wanting to worry you."

"Oh Richard," I said.

"Och well – don't worry I'm getting a bit fed up with the navy anyway. I'm thinking of leaving when my four years are up. I don't see me getting very far. All I can do is communications. I've been offered training for another job, welfare officer for the sailors. I would get special training. They think I would do well at that. I get on well with the lads and can look after their interests. But I've declined – no fear. One of the lads in the next bunk to mine never reappeared after the last trip. I found out it was because he had just murdered his wife. I'm not getting mixed up with that lot!"

Richard went on one more trip. This time to Bodrum in Turkey.

"It's yesterday," he said, "wonderful, eastern. I did like being there. I'd love to go back some time under my own steam, not with the navy. You can only see so much when you're in the navy."

His enthusiasm whetted all our appetites for seeing the world. Richard left after his four years and went to Aberdeen, a town beginning to undergo an oil boom and got a job working for Shell.

> "It's the politicians that start the wars not the ordinary people."

Chapter 16

Michael

Michael's teachers had wanted him to stay on at school for another year to get enough qualifications to go to art college.

"Out of 1800 pupils he's the best one we've got," the head art master told us. But no. Michael was for leaving.

"I don't want to be cooped up in school any longer and at the end of an art degree what would I do anyway? I wouldn't want to teach or go into commercial art and what else is there? I'd rather keep art as a hobby I enjoy – do my own thing my own way,"

Nothing would dissuade him. Had he been keen himself I would have helped all I could as would his father. Not that we always liked, or perhaps understood, Michael's art work – a bit too gloomy often for me, sometimes rather horrific, sometimes abstract but there were times when something would delight my senses – his portrait of his sister Mahri dressed in a Victorian shot-silk narrow-fluted and wasp-waisted black dress. The face was perhaps not quite as skilled as it might have been but the rest was a dream – the lights and shades in the black dress and in the old red velvet curtains behind, the green of the round fishing float she held, the yellow glow of the lamplight – there had been an electricity strike at the time. I thought it beautiful, had it framed and put it in a place of honour. Once I asked him to do a few small pictures for one or two poems of mine.

"I don't know if I can," he said, "but I'll try."

"They're just right," I said to Michael when he had finished. "That's just the way I see it too."

One of his earlier pictures was the inspiration for one of my early poems. Over the farm we had two sets of pylons marching across the emerald land to the city on the horizon. I had never particularly liked them.

"Spoils the landscape a bit," I said, "but think of the light and heat it gives people." Michael's painting featured one or two of these pylons – slender silver towers rising from green fields bordered by ancient hawthorn trees heavy with flower. The whole ambience of the picture affected me.

"I'll never quite see pylons in the same way again," I said.

"What do you want to do then, Michael?" I said one day before he left school. "Go into the navy like Richard?"

"No, I want to get away from regimentation and I don't think I am quite so desperate to see the world as Richard is. Not yet anyway. I don't really know. Perhaps I like farming as well as anything – growing things."

"Do you want to work for your dad then? – we could do with you."

"Don't think it would work Mum, Dad and I."

I remembered the rows there were between the two of them when he was younger but things had changed recently. Michael had changed. No longer was he the one always getting into trouble or deliberately annoying people, making brother Ronnie go crazy with rage before he was twelve. Something had changed in Michael. He had become considerate of others, reserved. He had always suffered a little from deafness. The doctor said, "Heredity. Can't do much about it." It had always kept Michael a little aloof from the others.

"Besides," continued Michael, "it's coming up for hay time and you know how impossible it is for me to work in that rye grass hay because of my hay fever." Well I knew that he had always been a martyr to hay fever for as long as I could remember.

"What then? You'll need to do something."

"I think I'd like to get a job far away on the west coast where they don't grow so much rye grass." I thought this was a bit of a dream but said nothing.

"Go ahead then," I said. "See what you can get."

My attitude to all the children was very much the same. What I most wanted was that they should do something they wanted to do that would give them enough to live on and be happy. Michael was a bit of a dreamer or perhaps all teenagers are.

The lines of Rudyard Kipling's – much maligned by poetry academics but loved by ordinary people – were a guiding light to me in my attitude to the children as they grew into adulthood.

If you can dream – and not make dreams your master;
If you can think – and not make thoughts your aim;
If you can meet with Triumph and Disaster
And treat those two impostors just the same;

I told them it was good to dream but they had also to be practical. For dreams to come true they had to be worked at. I told them that winning and losing weren't the most important things in life. From time to time they would do both. What was important was their attitude towards them and that if they lost they could rise again in some different way. How much they took in of what I said I had no way of knowing. They didn't say much.

Michael got a job on a farm in the west – packed up a few things and left without ceremony. A couple of weeks later I got a phone call.

"You'll never believe this. The farmer I'm working for gets his hay seed, rye grass, from one of your neighbours. It's in the air. It's everywhere. I can't stop sneezing and tomorrow we start cutting. Job's fine otherwise but I don't quite know how I'll cope. The farmer knows about my hay fever – can't avoid knowing. Maybe he'll give me another job."

"Come home then Michael," I said.

"No, I'm going to try and stick it out. Besides he needs me. He'd have a problem getting someone else at the last minute."

When the farmer demanded that Michael turn all the hay with a pitchfork, he found it impossible to carry on. His whole face swelled up till he could hardly see out of his eyes. His nose started to bleed, not in small measure but like mountain waterfalls. The farmer had no other job for him. He was forced to leave.

It took a few weeks of staying indoors before he recovered his health.

"What now Michael?"

"Well I've been thinking perhaps I should go into some other form of business."

"Such as?"

"Don't really know – making things."

"You've got to know something about business," his father said. "How about business college for a year or so."

"I could try it."

And so he went to business college in Dundee which was to stand him in very good stead later in life.

Afterwards a job came up in a factory in Dundee that made nuts and bolts. A year there and Michael had had enough.

"The money's not bad. I've made enough to go on a trip to Norway which I've always wanted to see. But I can't stand being inside day-in day-out for a moment longer."

> "For dreams to come true they had to be worked at."

When he returned from Norway he got a job in the forestry planting trees up in the highlands of Perthshire. He got lodgings with one of the McDonald clan who still didn't speak to the Campbells over the road. "The massacre of Glencoe," his landlady said to him, "It was a terrible thing to do, you know," just as if it had happened the day before yesterday. Memories are long in the Highlands. It was a lovely part of the world to be in and he enjoyed going out to plant trees every day. He joined the young farmers club. There was a lot of fun going on. He bought an old jalopy, couldn't really do without one. Occasionally there was an SOS to get him out of a fix. Once, one dark night he ran into a deer crossing the road, a common occurrence up there. His jalopy was a write-off. He had to get himself another.

After a year or two working for the forestry he began to see the job wasn't getting him anywhere. To get on in the forestry, have a regular job with decent pay, it was necessary to go to forestry college.

"Well why don't you?"

"Don't have enough qualifications for one thing but it's very difficult to get into. They've a huge waiting list."

"What do you want to do then?"

"Don't know – something outside though. I think I'd like

85

something with a bit harder work – more challenging."

"What do you mean – harder work."

"This planting trees once you get used to it is a bit monotonous and it's happy valley a bit."

"Happy valley?"

"Well being a government thing, there's a lot of going by union rules. It rains a bit and your off sitting in the van till it stops. I'd prefer to work on but you can't. You'd fall out with your buddies if you do that. Once or twice they've shouted at me to stop when I was up a hill. Being a bit deaf I don't always hear them and they're not very pleased to have to come and get me."

I had an idea. "What about your Uncle John." My sister-in-law Pat had lost her first husband in a car crash. Several years later she married John. John was a tattie merchant. He was a nice man. Working at tatties all the time Michael wouldn't have the hay fever problem.

Michael did go to work for his uncle and had no complaints about not working hard enough.

"I'll always be grateful to Uncle John," he said at a later date. "He taught me how to work."

Chapter 17

Ronnie

As a teenager, young Ronnie was in some ways one of the more rebellious. Rather than spend much time studying he preferred the excitement of the company of his friends in the village and liked nothing better than to get on his bike and be off to join his peers. Not that they did much, or so it seemed to me – a lot of standing around at street corners watching those who were lucky enough to have motor bikes roar up and round the Village Cross in flurries of exhaust fumes. Even on cold winter evenings you would see them in bunches standing against the cold Co-op wall opposite the pub – the territory they couldn't wait to be eligible to enter.

Not far from the pub stood the 'Chippy'. The boys, those with some pocket money left, would make quick breenges across the road for a can of Coke and a greasy poke of sizzling hot chips dispensed by Chippie Jean who would stand no nonsense from the boys. If there was any, she had no hesitation in telling them what was what.

Always there were one or two boys who were more trouble than others and had influence over the less adventurous. There could be sporadic trouble from these lads for several years until they settled down. But always there were others growing up to take their place. Rarely did anyone get into lasting trouble – the village saw to that. Gossip in a small community can be of value. News would seep through of whose laddie was doing what.

From time to time, down on the farm, we would hear rumours of what was going on. For a while teenagers were being accused of swearing at the back of the bus on their way back from the pictures in Dundee. Of course all mothers would say, "It's no my laddie. He widnae dae that!"

Actually our boys weren't particularly given to swearing, at least not in front of their elders. "You can swear in the barnyard if you like," their dad had always said to them. "But not in the house and not in front of strangers." Oddly his advice about smoking was the opposite.

"For goodness sake, if you're going to smoke, smoke in the house where I can see you. I don't want you burning the barn down." Consequently very little smoking went on. What was the pleasure, if it was not secret and forbidden?

The next thing the boys in the village were accused of was the throwing of stones. What laddie hasn't thrown stones at one time or another? It began with the gospel hall that one summer was set up in the Errol Park It was a wooden structure with windows. The hot gospelers invited the teenagers into the hall. This was something knew. The lure was free Coke and crisps and perhaps some games. Everything went fine until the hot gospelers one evening overdid the hell fire and damnation bit. Perhaps the teenagers got frightened. They all trooped out after the service and one or two threw stones at the hall. One boy broke a window. The hot gospelers were extraordinarily angry about this. A neighbouring farmer said, "What a fuss to make. Did St Paul no stone Stephen shortly before he saw the light? – become a Christian. I thocht that's what Christianity was a aboot."

The next time the boys were caught throwing chuckies about one accidentally hit the bottom pane in the village telephone box and cracked it. Most of us thought a sound telling-off by the village bobby (there was one at that time) would have been sufficient punishment. But no, they brought an inspector down from Perth and made a major issue of it.

Around this time Ronnie was fifteen and determined to leave school. We were disappointed as Ronnie had been one of the clever ones and in the days just before comprehensive schools had earned a place in Perth Academy. Only three or four graduated there from Errol per year. Father Ronald had recently insisted on our youngsters leaving school with some qualific-ations. Ronnie had none.

"I've an idea," he said to me one evening. "Let's see if Ronnie'll consider going to Elmwood agricultural college. He's the most keen on farming so far. He's been most conscientious with those breeding sows he bought with his own pocket money. Remember how he rang up every day from school at lunch time from a telephone kiosk to see how they were when they were farrowing. He could get O levels there and learn something of farming at the same time "

Ronnie agreed to go to Elmwood

"Come to think of it," Ronald said to me later, "it might not be a bad thing. It'll change the pattern, get him away from that teenage nonsense that's going on up in the village. Give him something else to think about. He's a clever lad."

His father had been right. When Ronnie came back from college with a few O levels he no longer sought the companion-ship of his former friends to the same extent – things had moved on. The pattern had been broken.

"What are you going to do now?" his father asked.

"Can I stay and work on the farm for a bit?"

Working on the farm for his father didn't last long. Both had too explosive a temperament. However with the wages he had made he was able to buy an old banger of a car and get his driving licence.

"Oh I don't know," he said evasively when I asked him about his plans. "I think I'll just blow, go further south. See if I can get a job on a farm if nothing else turns up."

His mind was made up. He set off early one morning, a dreich cool summer's day. I couldn't help worrying. He hadn't been driving long and his vehicle was an old banger. Worse, he didn't know where he was going.

"Ring me when you get to your destination," I told him.

I worried all day imagining all sorts of things. The phone rang in the early afternoon. I hardly recognised Ronnie's gruff voice. It was gruffer that ever.

"Mum, I'm in Hull. It's terrible weather here – a dense fog and there seems to be so many one way streets, I'm completely lost at the moment. To make matters worse I've developed a virus and don't feel too good but I hope to find somewhere to stay for the night soon. I'll phone you later when I'm settled – thought I better phone when I saw a phone box – thought you might be worried."

I had to think quickly before his money ran out.

"All right Ronnie. Find somewhere to stay for the night and phone me to let me know where you are. Make your way home tomorrow and stay here until you've recovered. Then you can start again."

Waiting for the next phone call was agonising. It came at midnight. Never had I been so relieved to hear anyone's voice.

"Ronnie, where are you?"

"I'm okay," his voice was a little clearer. "I'm at a pub in a village outside Hull. The landlady's very kind. She's given me a hot toddy and a room for the night. I'll phone you tomorrow – let you know my plans."

Ronnie didn't come home. He stayed for a few days in that pleasant inn and then took to the road again. He changed direction and landed in Appleby where he got reasonable lodgings for a week. He bought a local newspaper, went through its small ads and found a job on a sheep farm. It was wonderful countryside and Ronnie liked the animal side of farming. In his spare time he read a lot and after working for a year decided he would like to go back to college. There were courses in psychology in a college in Carlisle. He enrolled

He stayed a year at college and came back a different person. He had grown his red hair long – which I didn't think suited him one little bit. His jeans were patched and his t-shirts garish. With this new rig-out went new ideas. Strange ideas to us country folk – urban ideas – radical ideas – the talk was of communes and communities – a new society where everyone would share and share alike.

It wasn't until a much later date that he said one day, "You know why communes don't work?"

"No why?"

"It's the women's fault – they simply can't share a kitchen!"

After returning from college Ronnie had no particular idea what he wanted to do, other than to make enough money to travel and thus increase his knowledge of the world. Fortunately by this time Richard had left the navy and bought a flat in Aberdeen. This was to become a useful rendevous for most of the family. Work might have been scarce in the rest of Scotland but in Aberdeen, during the oil boom years, it was not. It wouldn't matter what the job was, Ronnie would attempt it as long as it paid good money. He was a hard worker and he could stay with Richard. And once he had saved enough Ronnie was off on his travels again.

"Where are you going to this time?" I asked him.

"Dunno exactly – France – Spain – Morroco – maybe end up in Greece. Expect me when you see me."

By the rattles and bangs it made I didn't think that the old car he planned to travel in would take him further than the bottom of the farm road.

"Could we not help him a bit to get something better?" I suggested to his father.

"No leave him alone. Let him find out the hard way. Don't mollycoddle him," was the answer.

So off Ronnie went rattle bang, rattle bang. I was wrong. The car did get him, albeit with some difficulty and several minor repairs, over the Pyrenees. Before crossing to Morocco he gave the car away to a young hitchhiker. It still had some life in it.

It wasn't till long afterwards that I heard about the scrapes the young people got into abroad. They appeared to have the grace never to tell me at the time. I would have been worried sick. I did however develop a sixth sense when something went wrong for any of them but which one, what was wrong or where, I had no idea. It was a useless sense in that I could do nothing about it, only have this awful sinking feeling. Comparing dates afterwards, the times were pretty accurate. Mother had always believed in telepathy. I did now too.

In Morocco Ronnie was bitten by a mad dog. He found it almost impossible there to get adequate medical attention but he didn't come home, rather carried on to Greece. Fortunately the dog hadn't had rabies and the wound healed.

On these long jaunts, like many of the other young hitchhikers, he got jobs to keep him going in olive or almond groves or picking whatever fruit was in season. When work was scarce he came back home to get a job to earn enough to go away again.

Next time he went off, it was to India and came back with extraordinary tales of a different place.

91

"What a tremendous country it is," he told us – so very different from here that there isn't really language to describe it – the mass of people, the poverty, the dirt, the overcrowded trains we travelled in, the sunshine, the cheerfulness, people living all their lives on the streets, raw humanity exposed. And Nepal is something else. You have to see the landscape to believe it."

He showed me photographs. There was something about the colours and contours that got to me.

"You would like it," he assured me

After his first visit to India he told a story of how he and his fellow traveller had to pay in advance for airline tickets to return home. The travel agent who took the money told them they could pick up the tickets when they came back for their flight the next day. When they went to do so, they were told by the same man that the tickets were not available. He had gambled their money and lost it all.

"Very sorry – come back tomorrow and I get the money and have your tickets – I promise." They were not available the next day. Ronnie protested, "We have no money left to stay here any longer." He threatened to go to the British Embassy.

"Don't do that," pleaded the official, "I tell you what I do. I give you a thousand rupees. It's all I've got. You go for three weeks up to Mussoori. It is a hill station above Delhi. You can live there cheap. Come back in three weeks. I have tickets – I promise. And that is what they did.

"Like living out of time, living in Mussoori," Ronnie said, "in this place where once a lot of British people had lived. None are there now but they have indelibly left their presence on the place. It is more like an English village than an Indian township. Walk down the quiet streets to find cottages with roses growing up the walls. The monsoon had started and it seemed at times as if we were living in a cloud which would occasionally open to show us the whole plain of India below us. Very strange and powerful."

"And what happened?"

"In three weeks we went back to Delhi. The Indian official had our tickets. We flew home. What a relief that was. I don't know what we would have done. There are people who get stuck in India forever."

The one thing Ronnie never seemed to think of doing was phoning home to ask for help. I would have liked him to but his father was proud that he didn't.

Ronnie came back from India thin but fit enough. He worked at home for a while to make some money again. It was the busy season on the farm. He was still with us when the students came back to the bothy in October. Now that our boys were much the same age as the students they often became friendly with them, especially Ronnie. Whenever there was a party going over at the bothy he was there. Like his dad before him Ronnie was good at parties – very witty and funny and could get a heated argument going, but could control it also. After having been at college in Carlisle he could speak the students' language. He was a man of his time, to them deliciously radical. Perhaps the students envied his lifestyle – a free man taking off where and when he liked – a free thinker.

"In tomorrow's world there will be no characters left," said one of the student's one evening.

"Oh yes their will," said another

"Who – who will be the characters of tomorrow? We are all put in such straight jackets of work and careers."

"Well Ronnie for a start," was the instant answer.

That particular year Lord Mackie was put up as the only candidate for Rector of Dundee University. Lord Mackie was well on in years – had always been a respectable citizen, had made money and enjoyed a certain amount of fame. His ideas were the opposite of radical.

"Boring," said the students, "must get someone to stand against him – someone nearer our own age who will at least give him a run for his money – but who?"

One of our students had a bright idea. "How about Ronnie? Full of ideas is Ronnie on changing the world, and just back from India. That's the place to be these days – and he looks radical – long straggly hair, patched jeans."

"It's really quite a lot of work being as scruffy as this," Ronnie said to me one day while sewing, rather ineptly, yet another patch on to well-worn jeans which already had more patch than original material.

"Would you do it Ronnie?" asked the students. "We'd help you do most of the slog. You'd just be the front man."

"Well," said Ronnie, rather reluctantly, just so long as I don't win. I don't want to be Rector. As soon as I've saved up enough I'm off to Australia – intend getting a year's work permit – might stay there, who knows?"

"There's not much likelihood of winning but it certainly would give some excitement to the campaign. We'll need to give you a high profile. The powers-that-be won't like it. Be prepared for strong opposition."

The whole idea didn't appeal to me but who was I? – only mother. My opinion was not sought.

The campaign began. Large posters appeared everywhere in the vicinity of the university, either with huge letters stating GILLIES IS GOOD FOR YOU, or with pictures of a large nose big letters underneath saying RONNIE NOSE. Neither the students or Ronnie had much money to put into the campaign so they had to be inventive. Recently work had been done on the roof of an outhouse on the farm. New slates had been put on. There was a pile of the old slates stacked against the barn wall.

"Could I have some of them, Dad?" Ronnie asked.

The old slates, along with a pieces of chalk, were taken to the university and put on display with a placard stating they were 'Revolutionary calculating aid slates.' Big queues of students formed eager to have one.

The only time Ronnie asked me for anything came later in the campaign.

"Could I have a dozen jars of your raspberry jam?" he asked me one morning. They stood glowing on a top shelf in the kitchen – ruby legions of them.

"What on earth do you want them for?

"Lord Mackie is giving the students free pies and pints. I must give them something. The students at the bothy suggested 'jam pieces'. They love your raspberry jam. It'll be something different – unexpected.

Ronnie began to gain ground. Every student, it seemed, was wearing a large round disc with VOTE FOR RON in large letters. They came flocking to his speeches which would be revolutionary, I've no doubt, although perhaps a little tongue in cheek. Witty I knew they would be.

"Look, cool it lads," said Ronnie one day to his student friends. "I'm not wanting to win this thing."

But the university was getting worried and I didn't blame them. Some student undercover agent came across a letter. The university was investigating Ronnie and had written to the college in Carlisle to see if they could get anything against him. Back had come the note.

"He didn't do anything wrong, he didn't join any communist or radical party. But some of the crowd he ran with . . ."

Ronnie got three quarters of the number of votes gained by his opponent. He heaved a sigh of relief – now he was free to go to Australia.

Chapter 18
The Market Place

Ronald's health was not improving. The circulation in his legs was giving him problems. He tried to ignore this but he took to using a stick – the smartest stick around. He had several with beautifully carved heads – a deer, a spotted trout, a dog. When he saw an unusual stick he bought it and began to make a collection. His problems with health did not alter his neat appearance. He had never gained weight, clothes sat well on his slim frame – he often wore a tweed jacket and hat that suited him and when going out, even to the market, he always wore a bow-tie.

"Always tie my own," he would tell any farmer who, thinking it was one of the elastic type, would try to make it ping.

He was still very independent and it was hard to believe he wasn't well. I could help with the driving and took him about wherever he needed to go. Once a week, to the market, was a regular excursion. In those days there was still a lot of business done at the market. This was the day the farmers got together, bought and sold animals and crops, bought from the salesman, bargained, exchanged information, gloomed over weather and prices. A Friday afternoon was the main market day. It had been customary for some time for a farmer and his wife to go in together, the wife to shop, perhaps meet a friend.

The market was the farmers' domain. Wives didn't enter unless to collect husbands and even then it was a dangerous thing to do. He might not have finished some lengthy negotiation. You were better not to interrupt. However Ronald didn't mind me coming to collect him at the end of the day in the market bar, and I came to enjoy entering this male province. I found it immensely interesting. I loved everything about it – the odd mixture of smells – rain, dung, tweed jackets, wet raincoats, and the men in country clothes topped usually by a cap or, in the case of the farmers from further north, by a deer stalker with flaps to keep their ears warm. There was a healthy atmosphere about – the smell of outdoors, the wind, the rain and the sun-growing crops. All of this was mixed of course with the smells of whisky, beer and cigarette smoke that rose like clouds over a hillside, and the main noise – the babble of men's voices, the explosion of laughter from time to time to which Ronald contributed often with his ready wit and his quick grasp of the ridiculous.

> "Many farmers are living on borrowed money – a bank has just to foreclose. It's a constant worry."

There was hard bargaining too. Deals were done with the shake of a hand – no signature needed, nothing other than perhaps the luckpenny, money that changed hands for luck, it was said, an old custom of the market place.

There were all kinds of farmers of course, just like there are all kinds of people in any walk of life. There were the greedy and the generous – happy and dour – rich and poor – so poor were some of the hill farmers that they would be living on less than the dole. They all mixed together as one, understanding each other's problems. No farmer was too cocky about what he was earning because he knew that next year his earnings might be drastically reduced. You could never tell. There could be a run of good years when the weather behaved and prices were good but you knew that it was inevitable a run of bad years would follow when the weather refused to be anything but inclement, the prices poor, the government and the people against you, but you travelled on. Perhaps it has always been so.

In the poor years Ronald would say, "I don't really know why men want to be farmers. Those who own their land would make a lot more money if they sold up and put it into shares."

I tried to reason it out. "Perhaps it is the sense of freedom that farmers have. They think they are their own bosses even although it's a complete fallacy."

"Yes," said Ronald, "farmers must do whatever the market and governments dictate – they must follow the party line to keep alive at all. If governments say produce something cheaper you have to put on your thinking cap – cut out every little expense. You don't always produce better food that way but you've got to do it or go down and that's not hard to do. Many farmers are living on borrowed money – a bank has just to foreclose. It's a constant worry. Look at this new barley beef racket. You might just make enough to live on feeding barley to the cattle but the meat does not taste as good as when they were fed on neeps and hay. And take tatties – these new varieties give a better crop but do not taste the same."

"Maybe it's the love of the land, that keeps farmers farming," I suggested.

"Well, maybe," replied Ronald, "especially if that land has been handed down through grandfather, father, son – it gives a sense of permanence, belonging which you didn't find to the same extent in Canada where farms are so new. Farmers there would sell up at the drop of a hat."

Was farming such an elemental thing for a man to do? Is he being truly himself in providing what's necessary for life. As with anywhere in the market place there is jockeying for position, competition. The survival of the fittest, who will survive, who won't.

I loved to listen to the snippets of discussion that got up among farmers. Who ever said they were not clever? A bit slower than town people perhaps, but clever, astute when they needed to be. In the Spring time an influx of Irish dealers could be found in the market bar selling cattle from Ireland to fatten on the sweet lush grass of the Carse. Ronald bought cattle every Spring. He usually bought them from an Irishman. The thin but rangey cattle he had for sale did well on the good grass of Inchmichael. Ronald was never quite sure if he had paid too much for them or not. What would the price be at the end of the day?

"Ach well, if I've got to be cheated," he would say, "I'd rather be cheated by an Irishman. They do it so nicely."

Ronald loved the ready wit of the Irish and their charm. "Charm a bird out of a tree, they can," he would say.

Ronald used to say to me from time to time, "If anything happens to me you may have to sell up especially if none of the boys want to come and farm. It's too difficult for a woman. It's a man's world."

I didn't altogether agree. My mother had taught me from an early age a woman can do anything. It had sunk in.

"I've left it so that you'll have the life rent – saves double tax that way and then all seven will have an equal share – but no way could seven live off the farm – it would probably have to be sold unless you could think of doing something different, but what?"

If anything happened to Ronald, God forbid, I would have no desire to be a farmer – I'd had a ladleful of it. There seemed little place for women in this world. There were some women farmers but I think they had a pretty tough time of it. One I heard of was in pigs and from time to time had to go to the market to buy pigs. She was nicknamed Boar Annie. I had no wish to be called Boar Maggie.

Chapter 19

A Special Gathering

The practical necessity of the market place was one part of my life but running parallel with it was the other side – the dream, the introspective seeking to make sense of things. Poetry helped to fulfil this role. Any part of the day or night when I could get a spare moment was devoted to this in some way or another. It involved also the religious path I was on. From time to time they came together. My meditation, although perhaps I didn't realise it at the time, was done on the long solitary walks I took when I could round the farm. No matter what the time of the year, I loved those walks – the getting away – the freedom if even for only a short while – the wind in my hair, the rain in my face, tingling frosty fingers, the sun.

I loved to watch the other occupiers of this land – the wild flowers bordering the pow, each in their different seasons; the thousands of greylag and pink foot geese feeding in our fields in winter; the air filled with lark song in Spring; the coming of the curlew and oyster catcher to their nesting grounds, the swallow to its barn; deer leaping our ripening crops and the hares in congregation playing mad games – I loved seeing them all.

I was also now reading whenever I could – other poets, philosophers, religious men – Eckhart trying to bring religion together, the Christian mystics, Bhuddist, Zen Bhuddism, some aspects of which I felt I could identify with, Carl Gustav Jung (whom I still think is much underestimated). Whatever book I could lay my hands on.

By this time I had had a lot of poetry published in magazines, anthologies etc. and although I had never met him, I had three collections done by Howard Sergeant. And not having met him was to change. One of the other poetry magazines I took, called *Pause*, had a real entrepreneurial editor – a man with good ideas.

100

He hatched the idea of a special weekend to be held in Birmingham where prizes would be given out to two sections of the poetry world. One for the person who, in the eyes of a carefully selected panel of judges, was seen to be the most fitting to win the prize, one who over the years had done the most to forward poetry and help up-and-coming poets. The other prize was for the best poem written by someone between the ages of 16 and 18. It was to be an annual event. That year Howard Sergeant was to win the prize for the poet who had been the most help to others. A girl from Edinburgh won the prize for having written the best poem. The Victorian edifice of the Grand Hotel in Birmingham was the chosen venue.

I wanted to go. For one thing, here would be my chance to meet Howard Sergeant and other poets. It was to be a big gathering. Ronald didn't like not having me around but agreed that I should go. He liked to encourage what he saw as my hobby when he could. It was all arranged and Mahri came with me.

As far as I was concerned it was a most enjoyable weekend. Mahri thought so too but for different reasons. Although she liked poetry she had no great interest in it but as she was a pretty girl some of the poets made quite a fuss and were kind to her. She was a shy girl and her years around leaving school had been difficult. This attention was good for her bruised ego.

For some reason I felt that Howard Sergeant would hardly know me even though he had published three collections of mine. To my astonishment he knew all about me. I didn't realise how much a publisher does know through reading the work of the people he publishes. All I ever had had from Howard were brief notes, often comments telling me where I had gone wrong. At the gathering he didn't have much time to talk to me as he was much sought after. It was a very full weekend which I found most interesting.

Most people left on Sunday afternoon but because of transport arrangements, Mahri and I had to wait till Monday. The other people staying over on Sunday night were Jonathon Clifford, the organiser and editor of *Pause*, the winners of the competitions, one or two other poets, and the Duchess.

The Duchess was an American lady married to an Italian

Duke. She was a poet, a friend of Clifford's but also, it was rumoured, she was to help to pay for this glorious event in the Grand Hotel.

After dinner the remnants of the 'get-together' met in the sumptuous bar complete with marble pillars. For a while the Duchess dressed in flowing silk kept us all amused with the fantastic stories of her life. Mahri got into conversation with the girl who had won the poetry prize and her mother who had come with her as chaperone. Howard was sitting on my other side.

"Well Margaret, and where do you think your poetry's going from here?" he asked.

After that question there took place one of the most interesting discussions I had ever had. It was something that I very much needed. I was coming to the climax of the long religious path I had been on since an argument I had with the church fourteen years previously over the christening of Kathleen. I needed someone to talk to. I never dreamed it would be Howard but he was the right person. He had a deep understanding of people's inner needs. Also having once, when young, seriously thought of becoming a Methodist minister he could understand what I was talking about and it was understanding that I needed more than anything else – being listened to rather than being given advice – everyone has to work out their own solutions.

Howard did this service for a lot of his poets, I think. He was a man with a wealth of understanding and a dedication to poets and to the dream of his own poetry. The rest of the people in the Grand Hotel that Sunday evening, sitting round the old oak bar table, faded into the marble pillars. I'm not sure how long we talked nor can I remember exactly what was said but what I do know is I was gently led on to the right path for me and this was to help me greatly in the difficult years that were to follow. That was the only long conversation I ever did have with Howard. It was enough. It may have been an hour, it may have been half an hour before Mahri plucked my sleeve.

"Mum. It's after midnight. Is it not time we were off to bed?" The Duchess had already gone unnoticed by me. She stayed in the Grand Hotel for another three weeks, I learned later, and left without paying her bill!

Chapter 20

Homecoming

The farm that once had required a lot of men to work it now needed only two. Ronald had pursued his low cost policy of farming – few animals – not too big a diversity of crops – some land let to merchants for peas and potatoes. For the past few years we had been left with two men but now Dave Scott was of retiring age and ready to give up. The boys were gathered together and a farming conference ensued.

"Someone will need to come home," said their father. "Either that or we'll sell up." Ronald had grown increasingly pessimistic about farming. "It doesn't matter how hard you try, it's never going to be anything else but difficult. You do very well for a while and then everything seems to go against you again – the weather – crop failure – the government. I'm tired. I don't feel like taking on a new man." As Richard was the eldest, he asked him how he felt.

"I'll think about it, Dad. Perhaps I'll give it a try. That's me finished at college now. With the qualifications it has given me I intended to look for a job in the merchant navy but I know it's going to be difficult. All these container ships nowadays – they're so big fewer crews are needed."

Within a week Richard had decided he would come back to the farm. "But I'll need a house of my own," he added. "I'm too old to be living with my parents any more. I've been too long away from home."

And there would need to be changes. He'd want to do things differently.

Ronald agreed this must be so. I could foresee problems just the same as there so often is in farming families between father and son.

"I'll keep my flat on in Aberdeen in case I change my mind.

103

I'll let it out in the meantime to any brother or friend that wants it. It's useful to have somewhere in Aberdeen."

Grant, number four son, thought this a good idea. Since leaving school he had been working off and on spasmodically on the farm feeling he would have to stay and help. Now he was free. He could have adventures like the rest of them – find out what life was all about.

The harvest was good that year. Things went well.

At the end of October a postcard came for Richard. I noticed the signature was Linda.

"A girlfriend," I said lightheartedly.

The boys didn't discuss their girlfriends much with me. Richard had never mentioned Linda.

"A girl I met when I was on holiday in Greece last year," was all that he said.

A couple of days later there came a phone call from London. It was Linda. She was coming up for a few days.

I looked forward to meeting this mysterious Linda, an Australian. It was bonfire night when she arrived. We had got into the habit every year of having a bonfire night for the young folk. We never held it exactly on the 5th of November so that all their friends would come from the village and not be distracted by any other bonfire.

It was always a night of excitement – a huge blaze from wood and rubbish collected over the year – a falling guy consumed by flames, fireworks, sparklers twinkling in the air, excited voices and the smell of hot sausages and potatoes in the dark November air. I was busy in the kitchen when Linda arrived, filling the ovens with baked potatoes and apples for the evening feast. Richard brought her into the kitchen – an attractive twenty year old with long dark glossy hair that had a natural wave, big brown trusting eyes and the kind of face, Ronald said afterwards, you find on a Greek icon. Linda's origins were Yugoslavian, both her parents having originated from there. She was different but we liked her immediately.

Linda remained for more than a few days. At New Year they announced their engagement. I had guessed that's how things were going. Ronald and I were delighted. The day after the announcement I wrote to her parents in Australia. I had wanted to before. They will be worrying, I thought, what's happening to their daughter up here in dark Scotland. The wedding was arranged for June. Linda had decided she would like to have it in Scotland.

"Nothing but the best," said Ronald. "The George Hotel in Perth. Seeing her folks have all the expense of coming here, I'll help pay for it."

Linda's parents came over to stay with us for six weeks before the wedding in order to get to know us better and help wherever they could. They had never been in Britain before.

"I could foresee problems just the same as there so often is in farming families between father and son."

Those were a busy happy six weeks. Linda who had a diploma in fashion and design made her own wedding dress – a simple pale-cream creation with an embroidered bodice worked by herself. I thought she was extremely clever to do this so quickly. She was good with her hands. Her parents brought all sorts of Australian touches to the wedding and made the cake. The day shone brightly on the sun-sparked river which ran in front of the hotel. It was a happy occasion.

With Richard taking on responsiblities back on the farm, Grant was now released and was off to Aberdeen. The leaving process of our fourth son, though, came as rather a bombshell.

Chapter 21

Grant

Not long before Richard decided to come back and work on the farm Grant had left school – determined to do so. He left with three or four O-grades and one or two unexceptional Highers – much the same results as the others had achieved and certainly not enough to go on to university. At one stage he had shown a special aptitude for physics which he could understand, but like the rest he had not studied hard enough. Not going on to higher education was no hardship for Grant. Home lessons had not been encouraged by his dad.

"Home lessons – you shouldn't have to have home lessons – a school day is long enough. If they can't teach you between these hours – well!!"

It was the wrong attitude for a father to have if he wanted his sons to go to university but I'd learned to say nothing. They had a happy life at home on the farm with always something to do, always some new excitement.

"What do you want to do then?" I asked Grant one day not long before he left school.

I got the usual answer. "Dunno, I'll see." Grant was a youth of few words with a detached air, although that may have been deceptive. He had always seemed laid-back and happy enough, an easy lad to bring up. He had always got on well with his father as he wasn't given to arguing.

"Honest John," Ronald used to call this handsome son of his with the broad shoulders, deep brow and the calm eyes. He could be stubborn and it was difficult to get information out of him, difficult to know what he was thinking. He helped on the farm for a short while before his brother came home but underneath he wanted to get away – like the other Gillies boys he wanted adventure.

"I think I'll go up to Aberdeen. See if I can find work," he announced one day and was gone. Aberdeen had become a sort of second home to the family with Richard having his flat there. A lot of their friends congregated there too. There was many a party in Aberdeen at the weekends. Grant got a job through Giant, a labour hire firm used by oil companies. He saved every penny he could. He was a good saver. After about nine months he came home for a weekend.

"I'm off to Canada," he said, "next week." Both Ronald and I got a shock – there had been no mention of it until that point.

"You're only just eighteen," I said.

He explained that he was heading for the town of his birth – Edmonton.

How long did he mean to be away for? What was he going to do there?

"Dunno," was the laconic answer. "But there's this Canadian girl, Teresa that I met in Aberdeen. She's from Edmonton, said she could get me a job okay. Lives just outside Edmonton on a quarter section of land with five other girls – I only met her recently but she seems genuine enough and helpful. We got talking one evening. When I heard she came from Edmonton I mentioned that was where I was born. 'Have you ever been back?' she said. 'Nope,' I said. 'Why not?' she said. 'Haven't had the opportunity.' 'What would you like to do?' I couldn't think of anything special to say so I said travel. Where to? – well why not Canada. We discussed it a bit. 'Are you still a Canadian citizen?' she asked. As far as I know. 'You'll be able to get a dual passport if you hurry. There's talk of doing away with them but it means you will always be able to work in Canada if you have one.' Seemed like a good idea. I want to go somewhere different and none of the boys have been in Canada and you've always talked of it – the wide open prairie – the sunshine – the extreme cold – the wildness of it all – the sort of place I might like."

In no time at all he was gone.

I worried remembering how difficult things could be in Canada. "Now remember always keep enough money to phone home if you get into any sort of difficulty." I had said this to them all but no one ever had.

It was a while before I heard from Grant and I had no address to write to him. I didn't worry about this unduly. I had got accustomed over the years to the boys being out of contact for long stretches of time, and I had so much at home to occupy my mind.

When he went, I asked myself why did Grant, of all the sons, choose to go back to Canada. Although he was unaware of it, perhaps the idea was there from the beginning. From the earliest of days he had heard tales of his birth in the northern city of Edmonton and of his journey to Scotland at nine months in a jet following the polar route. Perhaps when he played games with his brothers and sisters on the world map hanging on the kitchen wall, he noticed with more interest than the others, the frontier lands of northern Alberta that he had often heard us talking about. And he had learned from us, his parents, that Scotsmen had always gone seeking their fortunes in other lands, as if wanderlust was in their blood. His brothers had gone. He must do likewise.

His friend, Teresa's timing had only been the catalyst he needed. After a while there came a letter – quite a long one. One of Teresa's friends had driven him to Swan Hills about a hundred miles north of Edmonton to look for work. Swan Hills was a very new town built by the oil companies and was made up mostly of bunkhouses and trailers. There was also a bar – a mini supermarket, a general store, a Baco pizza parlour, a coffee shops and a RCMP Station. And the Swanhill area was famous for "Swanhill Grizzlies", a giant bear whose ancestors used to roam the prairies. The gun had nearly wiped them all out but they had survived in Swan Hills.

Within an hour of job seeking Grant had got work through a labour and tool hire firm, to begin with, digging holes looking for lost pipes. He was fairly useless at this – digging into virgin soil and permafrost was difficult and the guys that he worked beside told him he looked more like fifteen than eighteen. They got him out of the way by putting him on lookout so that he wouldn't get caught doing nothing. If he saw the boss coming he'd get into the hole again.

He stayed in a bunkhouse at night with three 'Nufies' – a strange tribe of Canadians, according to Grant, who come from the far north east – Newfoundland. The room he shared with the Nufies was very small – two sets of up and down bunks. One on the left and one on the right with about four feet in between. On the left as Grant described it, there was enough room for an oil-fired stove which had two settings – sweltering or arctic. The Nufies seemed to like the first setting and sometimes, at night, Grant found himself outside in the snow, gasping for air. However, after work, they often went out because of the cramped accommodation and and as often as not, found themselves in a bar .

"he had learned from us, his parents, that Scotsmen had always gone seeking their fortunes in other lands"

Later Grant got work with a firm called Tamarisk Plumbing and Heating. He wrote that he felt homesick but that work was the best cure. So he wrote about his work.

The name of my boss is Jerry. He's a big stout fellow who likes big game hunting as he calls it and also donuts. He has two brothers Vernon and Allan. They are stout also. Allan is married, so is Jerry. Vernon is single. They all live in various trailers about town. There is also Gary Byrne from Conche, Newfoundland who started work at the same time as me. We have a whole bunkhouse trailer to ourselves. It belongs to Jerry and he takes money off our wages for the rent. It is spacious compared to my previous place. It has a big living area and two bedrooms although we are asked to share the same room in case he is able to let it to men from the oil companies. In the living area there is a giant electric stove which I am told is quite a normal size for Canada, a table and two or three chairs. The bedrooms, which are situated one on either end of the living area, each have two home-made beds with plastic mattresses. The walls are fake wood panelling which is getting dingy. The window looks onto a giant porch which is attached to another trailer. The entrance into the bunkhouse is through the porch. At the far end of the porch are the showers and toilets. Then there is another bunkhouse complex and then Jerry's large workshop. It's all laid out to form a large court yard, car park. The bunk houses are one of Jerry's money making schemes. The complex is in a good situation at the entrance to Swan Hills with a gas station on one side and a coffee shop on the other, the Red Rooster.

Soon I hope to get a car – an old banger when I have saved enough money. You can't do without a car in this outlandish place. Everyone has one. You are not supposed to walk even here. You are thought odd if you do. On the first week I came here I was walking up the windy street of Swan Hills when I got stopped by the mounty (or rather a RCMP officer as they now like to be called). He drove up to me in his four wheel drive, a massive vehicle, and asked me in. He asked me questions, quite a grilling, where was I born, where did I work etc. I thought this strange as I had never been stopped before for walking up a street but it seems to be a mounty tradition in these parts to find out who strangers are and what their business is. He kept asking my age – said I looked about fifteen. Fortunately I was able to show him my passport which seemed to satisfy him. I think I'll try and grow a beard to make me look older. Since then I've met him once or twice. He's always very friendly and helpful.

We are doing the plumbing in a big new housing scheme up at the top of the town. On the first day I came Jerry took me up there and helped with the roughing in. I was useless and eventually he told me so. However he decided to leave me to it one weekend and I found I got on better without him at learning what to do and for the first time on arriving in Canada felt useful. After that he left me to it teaching me each new bit of the trade as the need arose.

Some of the jobs are a bit dodgy though. The water and sewer pipes have to be around eight feet deep as the frost goes down five or six feet. I have to work at the bottom of this deep ditch. I'd been told to watch for the ditch collapsing and that there is not much you can do when it does. A few weeks ago a big heap of sand fell on my back and buried my legs. Jerry dug like crazy and got me out. Don't worry Mum I'm much wiser now and will be much more careful and watchful.

We got some good moose meat from Jerry after his hunt. Jerry cuts up the moose meat in the workshop with a chainsaw. He also knows someone who has a sausage making machine. We all had moose meat sausages for ages. They were great.

More mother-worrying tales came in subsequent letters.

He eventually managed to buy his own car – a Chevrolet Impala – "all black, a great giant beast of a thing". Grant "thought it was a goner" not long after he got it.

One morning I got up looked out the window to find the snow had a more permanent look to it – like it was here for the winter – serious. It had been snowing and melting for some time but this looked different. I had my breakfast and then went out to start my car. The moment I walked out I got a shock. It was perishingly cold. I ran round to my car, jumped into the front seat. It didn't sink beneath me as it usually did. It had turned into solid ice. I turned on the ignition, the engine turned but a terrible noise came from it. It sounded as if it was full of gravel. Jerry asked if I'd plugged it in. Plug it in? What was he talking about? 'You have to plug it into the electricity when it's this cold or the water in the radiator freezes.' I'd wondered what the plug on the hood or, as we would say, the bonnet was for. Jerry showed me where to plug it into the mains. After two hours the car started like normal.

I went on that day to feel the coldest I've ever felt in

all my life. I'm totally unprepared for this first day of real winter. I think Canadians must be superhuman to handle this cold. I must be made for a warmer climate. Gary tells me I don't wear enough. I need more clothes.

Two months later, he wrote,

Not long after the cold set in for real Jerry took me to do some work on a roof. The wind was blowing and it was about 30^0 below. I could hardly get up the ladder because of the pain of that cold. When I got up to the top Jerry was looking around at the view apparently not noticing the cold while I cowered behind a chimney. He turned round, took one look at me and told me to get off that roof quick. Seemingly my nose had turned white which is what happens before frostbite sets in. He told me later the fact that not wearing a hood had a lot to do with it.

Since then the Nufies and I have been down to Edmonton several times. Driving there can be a problem. The first time was the worst – on the motorway going towards Edmonton on sheet ice. I had ignored Jerry's warming about bald tyres at this time of year. Getting into Edmonton isn't much of a problem. You just head for the skyscrapers which you see for miles. Getting out is more difficult. I was so sure you had to just head north and would not listen to my companion, who said west first then north. I did a lot of wandering about avenues and streets, crossed and recrossed the Saskatchewan River.

Every time on the way we would meet a moose on the road and I would have to slam on my brakes as I looked in awe at them. They are strange-looking creatures, alien to my eyes. I'll maybe give up the car. Cars can get you into trouble. It nearly did with me the other night. Or perhaps it's just Nufies that get you into trouble. They're nice lads – good and entertaining, but boy can they ever drink! No way can I keep up with

them. It's the custom to stand huge rounds of pints –
four and that's my lot but they seem to be able to drink
endlessly and they get a bit obstreperous when they get
really drunk.

One evening I was at a party with Gary and a few
others that I knew. Gary was trying to be friendly with
one of the Nufies but he must have said something that
displeased him. I never noticed. This particular Nufie
had a huge build. He looked like how I imagined a giant
would look. When we got up to leave he followed us
out with his brother, also a giant. He grabbed Gary by
the collar and with a big grin on his face one huge fist
after the other pummelled into him. Other Nufies
swarmed around trying to ease Gary's plight but were
kept at bay by his brother – couldn't get anywhere for
the flying punches. I went in trying to negotiate and
received a heavy blow on the stomach which doubled
me up. We finally broke away and got into the car.

Gary's face was bloodied and bruised. He was
determined that I would drive him to the police station.
I was none too happy about this as I had more drink
than I should have had. Nevertheless I drove him there.
The mounty who had picked me up and had asked me
all these questions when I first came to Swan Hills was
on duty. He asked us both questions. There was lots of
cursing and blasphemic descriptions from Gary as to
what had happened. The mounty took photos of his
face. When we got up to go he asked who was driving. I
told him I was. He thought a bit and then to my relief
said 'Drive straight home.' Don't worry Mum, I'm selling
my car.

Chapter 22
Mahri's Wedding

As it was with all of the children when they returned, what a delight it was to see Grant again after what seemed like an age away. What a welcome he got – all the family rallied round – there were parties, there were visits to the pub in the village. There was another cause for celebration also. Mahri-Louise was getting married. She had met a handsome young Black Watch soldier. Shortly he was to be posted to Germany for three years and they wanted to get married before he went. Ronald was delighted at the match but grumbled a bit.

"Richard's wedding last year. How can we afford another one so soon and moneywise last year was not a good year on the farm."

Because of his ill-health I spent a lot of time trying to solve problems and minimise worries on my own. At this point I did suffer a feeling of isolation. I felt there was no one I could talk to, no one with whom I could discuss my family problems. The young were either away from home or too young and with enough problems of their own just coming to terms with the responsibilities of life. The few older relatives still alive were too old to have them worry about things. I had no close younger relatives of my own – no brother and my one and only sister was dead. I had friends but perhaps like my father before me, I had difficulty expressing feelings to others. Besides, I was intensely loyal – I would have felt it was a breach of trust had I discussed the family's, or my sick husband's, or my own problems with another.

Release came however, one day after an especially worrying time. It was a wonderful Spring day with all the birds singing. I had escaped for a short time and was rambling round the greening fields when in a flash, from nowhere it seemed, words

came into my head – ' Thy will be done.'
Suddenly everything tumbled into place.
I had been thinking I could solve all the
family's problems and bring Ronald back
to health. If only I could do the right
things, find the right doctors. Now I
realised there was only so much I could
do, however hard I tried. Life in the end
was in the hands of other forces. I must
slacken the reins and live a day at a time,
just as I had done in those early days on
the lonely prairies of Canada. Tomorrow
was unforeseeable.

"Now I realised there was only so much I could do, however hard I tried. Life in the end was in the hands of other forces."

I felt much better after working this
out for myself. But I still felt the need of a
confidant who could help me in a
practical way with my problems. I could
think of no one.

However, as I had found so many
times before, someone always turns up. This time it was to be
my one and only sister-in-law in this country, Pat. I told her my
problem about Mahri's wedding.

"I've got an idea," she said. "You know the chapel attached
to your house. That would be just the very place to have the
reception. How many people were you thinking of having?"

"Around eighty," I said.

"Well it would be big enough. After the war sister Eileen had
her wedding at Inchmichael. It was a big wedding but they hired
a marquee as well. Put it on the lawn."

"I don't think I could cope with a bigger wedding," I said,
"not at the moment. We've discussed it and Mahri and David
are quite happy with a smaller one."

"The chapel's the very place then," said Pat, "couldn't be
more suitable."

The whole notion of a chapel attached to a farmhouse may
seem like a strange one to most people. For a large part of the
early nineteenth century the house had been occupied by the
Playfairs, tenants who farmed the land. The last Playfair died in

1875. The neighbouring farmer at West Inchmichael, Ronald's great grandfather, took over the tenancy of the land of East Inchmichael. He didn't need the house at the time, so the landlord let it to Bishop Germyne, a middle-aged man who may have been a friend or relative of the landlord, Lord Kinnaird who owned much of the land leading to Dundee. The middle-aged Bishop, retired from a post in Ceylon because of ill-health, soon recovered in the fresh air of Scotland. After the sudden death in 1876 of the Scottish Episcopal Bishop Forbes, Bishop of Brechin, he was offered the post. The good Bishop Forbes had lived in one room connected to Dundee's St Paul's Cathedral. There was no Bishop's house. Bishop Germyne elected to stay where he was and Lord Kinnaird, a devout man of good works, built on the chapel for him at East Inchmichael.

Bishop Germyne's wife was a bedridden invalid and part of the wall of her upstairs room was pushed through to form a doorway so that she could take part in the services. The chapel was used for several years for services until Lord Kinnaird built the Scottish Episcopal Church at Glencarse.

In 1908 Ronald's grandfather and family came to live in the house. Grandfather used the chapel for the reading of family prayers. When his son Ronald, a bachelor, inherited, being of a less religious and more practical nature, he used the chapel as a potato store. But when my mother-in-law came to live here things were different. She planned to use it as a beautiful drawing room for her own pleasure and for parties and gatherings. Because of World War II she didn't have many, but she had it done up in a baronial hall manner, making best use of the wooden wainscoting. She put in an enormous open fireplace above which hung a stag's head complete with antlers. On the opposite wall, french windows were pushed out to the green garden. A new oak panel floor was laid. Otherwise little else was changed. Windows still pointed heavenwards and the thick, curved, wooden beams were still in full view, vaulting towards the high apex of the roof.

I knew Pat and her daughters were expert at catering. Ronald was pleased with the idea. "The very thing," he said. "I would have suggested it but I didn't want you to be burdened with all the catering. That's good of Pat. She always comes up trumps when she's most needed. And the service can be at Kinnaird Church where Linda and Richard were married."

The minister was approached – the same good man that had christened Kathleen. He was only too pleased. A date was arranged. The fourteenth of December. We could not have known it was to be one of the coldest days of the century.

As always there were other unforeseen difficulties. Ronald had fallen and broken his leg a month beforehand and much to his annoyance had to be pushed up the steep incline to the small red sandstone church in a wheelchair – anathema to such an independent man. It was arranged for a few photographs to be taken of Mahri entering the church. It was such a pretty little church almost hidden among trees with hills and an old red sandstone castle in the background. Mahri, a picture in her long flowing white dress, almost froze and went up the isle shivering. How much this was due to nerves and how much to cold, we were never sure. A neighbouring friend and farmer was to play 'All for Mahri's Wedding' as the bride and groom emerged from the arched church door. Since his fingers froze, this proved impossible.

But once we got back to the farmhouse all was rectified. The heating had been on in the chapel for days. It was lovely and warm. The delicious buffet went without a hitch. Before midnight the bride stepped into the waiting car all done up with balloons etc. while the kilted groom was lifted sky high by his brothers-in-law and deposited in a barrow. After a quick hurl round the farm yard he was unceremoniously shoved into the car after his bride.

Apart from the wedding that was a bad winter. We had thought perhaps that the frost would be severe for a day or two and then disappear. But it stayed and it stayed. It was like being back in Canada. Half the pipes in the house froze. Poor Grant, who thought he had escaped from plumbing for good, found this was not the case. Everyone was in the same boat. There was not a plumber to be had in the district for love or money.

My father, now eighty-seven, was becoming frail. All of a sudden it seemed he had shrunk into himself. Also he had to go

117

into hospital for an operation for a hernia. When he returned he needed nursing. I made the sitting room, adjacent to the chapel, where such merriment had taken place only a short while ago, into a bedsitting room for him. My father and Ronald didn't get on all that well and since Ronald wasn't well either, it was a difficult time and I had to be diplomatic. The district nurse came down every other day to tend to my father and give him a bath. All the cold water downstairs was frozen. We had two water systems. The upstairs water wasn't frozen. So I had to trek down huge buckets of water from upstairs to the bathroom downstairs as my father couldn't go upstairs. Grant was not very complimentary about the Scottish plumbing. "This would never happen in Canada," he said. "Pipes running up the outside of the house wouldn't last one week in the winter."

My father died in March. It was very sad. Trying to look on the bright side I said to myself he was eighty-seven, had had a good life with very little illness and lived long enough to see a great granddaughter born.

Shortly afterwards Grant returned to Canada.

"I bought a return ticket, Mum, in case I decided to go back. I don't quite know what I'll do. Before I left I asked Jerry if I could have my job back. At first he said yes but when I got there he said no – I don't blame him. I did let him down and he's not a bad guy. I'm going north again though. There's more work further north and the place fascinates me." And so off he flew.

That was the last time he was to see his father.

Chapter 23

Loss

After my father died that Spring Ronald's health was increasingly giving concern. His broken leg had mended and he was out of his wheelchair but, because of the artery problems in his legs, found walking difficult. He wouldn't give up though, and went doggedly on.

Michael had come home late that summer after his adventures in America and Canada. Michael was at a loose end.

"How about staying at home and working with Richard?" his father had asked. Ben, the last of the men had come of retiring age.

"Two are needed to work the farm and I'm not able to do much physically these days. We've cut down the amount of hay grown and the amount of cattle for feeding. You just won't need to go near the hay or the cattle. Richard will see to them and we can get extra help in at hay time.

"Okay Dad, I'll give it a go." Richard and Michael got on pretty well together and their dad would be the boss. Michael, like his father before him was beginning to learn that the grass was not necessarily greener on the other side.

However well one is prepared for the death of a husband I think it must come as a great shock. I was prepared in one sense. Oh yes, I'd been told that his health was in a very precarious state by several doctors. In my mind I had faced the possibility even, but it's not he same as the actuality and even although he was a semi invalid, I didn't really believe he wouldn't go on living for a long time. Somehow or other I would keep him alive. But it was not to be.

In December Ronald began to have trouble with his chest. I got the doctor down. We had a new doctor now very different from the old Dr Edington, now retired, but like him compassionate and a very hard worker who loved his job.

"I think you will have to go into hospital for a day or two to have tests," he told Ronald.

"I'd rather not. I hate hospitals. Perhaps I won't come out again."

"Of course you will," said the doctor. "It's only for tests."

"I'm not going," said Ronald.

The doctor was most understanding.

"I'll see if I can get the consultant to come down here, bring his equipment." With that Ronald had to be satisfied. The consultant did come down with his equipment but unfortunately had the wrong plugs. He was not nearly so patient as our doctor. "My time is precious I don't have time to go changing plugs. You'll just have to come into hospital," and he was gone.

Reluctantly Ronald obeyed. Three days later he was dead. I couldn't believe it. I was devastated but somehow or other I managed to keep going over the funeral. I requested no letters. How could I possible face reading them – far less answer them? But here, as in many other things, I was wrong.

People wrote anyway. Letters were a comfort, praise of the loved one a solace. I got letters from people I hadn't heard of in years. I got letters from poetry people. Howard Sergeant wrote, "I send you not my sympathy but my understanding love." I found that, after all, I didn't mind writing back. Talking about Ronald, writing about him, kept him alive for a bit longer.

For ages afterwards from time to time I would forget he was not there and do things like set his place at the table. For someone who hasn't been through this it's hard to explain how it feels to have half of you gone. The half that you trusted and relied on. Now I was solely responsible for the welfare of the family – a daunting prospect it seemed. For their sake I would have to keep going.

And life went on. There were practical things that had to be done. In order to avoid double death duties I had been left the life rent. After me the farm was left between all the children. Ronald had not been able to see how otherwise he could be fair to them all. He had not thought it possible that we could go on with the farm. There were decisions to make. Family gatherings were necessary.

It was decided that the farm would continue. No reason why it shouldn't. Richard, Michael and I had all been made partners and because of that owned some of it. It was all very complicated. Lawyers could have made a hey day out of it.

"Your family is remarkable," said our family lawyer. "You all agree about things. Not one dissenter. Anything's possible where there is agreement and compromise." Through compromise it was agreed we would keep on the farm.

All these things and the everyday work helped to keep me sane but I found I had completely lost confidence. It was a struggle just to go out, even to the supermarket. Or driving even. And I couldn't trust myself – couldn't be sure that I wouldn't burst into tears. It had happened once or twice already – in the clothes shop when I gone to get a hat for the funeral – the floor girl who served me hadn't known what she'd done wrong when she said how nice of your husband to give you a hat for Christmas. Or in the butcher's shop when some one had been kind. Or more rarely when someone was being unkind, I had to be careful. I hadn't believed I could be so vulnerable.

On the other hand I loved to talk about Ronald and read some of the poems he had liked. One especially of Browning's, *A Woman's Last Word*. I read more of Browning – found solace and wrote poems also of my grief. Sometimes I even dared to read them out at writers' meetings. I've heard it said by people that they don't know how it's possible to do this but oddly, at the time, it's comforting, Keeping that person with you – not letting go is comforting. It can also of course be dangerous. One wrong word and the hurt goes searingly deep. I was most fortunate in my friends and fellow writers.

One day, a friend, a neighbouring farmer's wife, took me out to Dens Road Market in Dundee. I saw a bunch of beautiful knives there with lovely bone handles going for very little. I bought them. I remember thinking, what on earth am I buying knives for? I'll never use them – my life is over – no more entertaining or anything like that.

Gradually things improved a little. Sister-in-law Pat had a small get-together once a week and asked me along. This was always fun and it was safe.

One day after about three months I got a phone call. It was from Duncan Glen, the editor of one of the top Scottish poetry magazines, *Akros*. Recently I had started sending him work. I had been told by one well-published writer that it was useless sending him anything as he had enough good work for ten years worth of magazines – so I hadn't done so for five years until one day I thought I'll send some poems anyway and rather to my astonishment they were accepted. Since then I had been in contact quite a bit with Duncan. He had sent a very kind letter after Ronald died and now over the phone he was asking if I would consider putting a collection together. He would publish it. Would I like to come down to Nottingham where he was Professor and discuss it. Why not? I thought, and accepted his kind invitation.

I stayed with the Glens for four days. Duncan and Margaret, his wife, were kindness itself. I immediately took to Margaret – an attractive and busy lady who had been such a huge help to Duncan in bringing out *Akros* on a regular basis. She told me of their struggles in the early days when they had spent hours sewing the magazine together and had used the pram to transport them down to the Post Office. She had a party while I was there with different and interesting people. She took me to the pictures. It was *Ghandi* on the wide screen. I began to see there was light at the end of the tunnel and went home to work on the collection for Duncan that was to become *No Promises*.

Now, I was determined in my spare moments to throw myself into poetry. That was the year of the opening celebration of the Scottish Poetry Library, an occasion I will not forget. Snow had fallen in Edinburgh. I went with a friend – a rather frail friend. We walked together down a narrow Edinburgh lane to St Cecilia's Hall where it was held. We could have been back in the middle ages – the dimly lit street, the ancient buildings, the snow on the road and roofs and window sills. I told my friend to hang onto me so that she would not slip. It was me who slipped, fell all my length on the icy narrow pavement. But inside St Cecilia's Hall was warmth and happiness, haggis and whisky and Tessa Ransford, who was to make such a success of the library, leading proceedings.

It was in this year also that I met Brenda Shaw for the first time. Brenda was a lecturer at Dundee University. She was also a member of the university's writing group that Anne Stevenson had begun ten years or so before. She was editing at the time, the Seagate collection of poetry, poems by all who had connections with Dundee. She had written to Duncan Glen asking for permission to use certain poems and telling of her project. He had written back to say that a Dundee collection wouldn't be complete without some of my work being represented. Whereupon Brenda got in touch with me. I can always remember the first day I met Brenda standing on the steps outside Dundee University. I took to her immediately, felt a rapport. We have been friends ever since. She asked me to give a reading and talk to the university writers' group which I did. They were an interesting, diverse and friendly lot of people. Before the reading I was taken to a lunch high on top of the University Tower building with its huge windows and magnificent view over the rooftops of Dundee to the river beyond. Brenda invited me to join their group. They met on a Wednesday afternoon in a room at the university. I was already a member of two writing groups. I thanked them kindly and said I would love to join but I might not be a regular attender. However I became just that, had many happy hours in the company of the group and it was to become most helpful to me over the years.

That first year on my own also I made up my mind to attend one of the Avron Foundation weeks. I had heard quite a bit about the foundation that Howard Sergeant had helped to create. It had two centres in England, one in Devon and one in Yorkshire. It was the Yorkshire one I opted for. I chose a week before hay time. I'd go down by coach.

I liked travelling by coach and it didn't cost too much. I started off early in the morning and changed buses at Glasgow. At Manchester I had problems finding where to catch the bus for Hebden Bridge. On the map it had looked very close to Manchester. But no one I asked seemed to have heard of it let alone know where I should catch a bus that went there. Eventually I got there and changed buses again for the little village of Heptonstall. There I came to a standstill. There was still a couple of miles to go and I had a heavy case. I got a taxi. It was getting dark. The taxi dumped me unceremoniously in what seemed the middle of nowhere at the top of a steep stony track. "It's down there," the taxi-driver said. "Can't take you any further. It's too rough," and he was off into the night.

Perhaps I have never felt quite so alone as I did standing at the top of that track. Darkness was creeping in fast. I had to walk down, down, down that ravine in amongst these ghostly trees towards an immensely tall chimney that seemed to emerge from nowhere. I learned later once there had been a woollen mill there. An owl hooted eerily as I began to descend the path. Apart from the unnatural chimney I could see no other sign of habitation. Implanted in my mind was the picture in the brochure of an old stone house belonging to Ted Hughes standing on the right of the stony slope – no house there. I walked for what seemed quite a distance until I came to a corner. It was dark and it was eerie. I was frightened of what I might meet round that corner. What monster would I find?

I walked up the stony hill again dragging my suitcase. All was quiet on the country road – no traffic – nothing. What would I do? Be brave walk down again round that eerie corner? The place must be there somewhere. In trepidation but with resolve I walked down the stony track again, rounded the corner and there it was – the house on my brochure on the opposite side of the track, all lit and welcoming.

I got a big welcome when I entered. They thought I must have got lost – supper had been kept for me. The two course leaders were South African Jeni Couzin and Fife-born Adrian Mitchell. Jeni was starting the ball rolling even although it was late. Loosening us up she called it. Tarot cards were laid out. We had to pick one and let its message sink in – deep spiritual thoughts – I was tired by this time, confused. I picked a card – an archway. It reminded me of the archway into the garden at home so that was fairly easy although not very deep or spiritual.

I could feel that evening, the tension between the two leaders – Jeni so spiritual, Adrian so practical. I could feel his disapproval of Jeni's opening tactics. I wondered if this course was heading for disaster. In actuality they resolved their differences and agreed time about to do their own thing which actually worked very well. But that first night I had my doubts. I slept that night in a dormitory with six other women.

I was allocated a top bunk. A lady from Wales was below me. For some reason I was never to discover she took away the ladder. Five o'clock in the morning the alarm I had brought with me unfortunately went off. I must stop it before it woke the others – no ladder – no light. I made a resounding thump when I hit the floor. Everyone woke.

Not the top of the popularity poll, I dressed and crept out into the most glorious morning. The sun was just up and sparkling on the river – the trees were freshly green – the birds were singing as if Spring would never come to an end. The air was fresh and clear as it can only be as morning awakes. How different from the night before when all had been grim and frightening. I revelled in that morning walk.

Adrian took us a few walks after that around this sometimes bare and desolate spot – we were taken to the grave of Silvia Plath, Ted Hughes' first wife. It was difficult to be sad in the Spring sunshine. We all had to write on what we found on these walks – what they made us think of. Everyone wrote differently. Jeni had us enter into ourselves looking for truth. More difficult especially for the men. They were apt to come up with something funny and facetious, not that they couldn't have done what was wanted but they had no intention of giving themselves away. It seemed that women had not nearly the same level of inhibition as men in this respect. All in all, it was an interesting course and for a short while took my mind off other things.

And so ended the first year of widowhood.

Loss

There is this vast silence . . .
nothing more . . .
You should be here
In the kitchen – now!
With the offspring gone to bed,
Sitting in the high Windsor
That is so much a part of you.
You should be here
On this fire-out summer evening,
Drinking a last draught from banded mug,
Discussing this and that,
Wondering if the peas are ready to combine,
Asking if the yellow canary
In the window, the trailing fern, need water
Or how many of the
Speckled courgettes, glossy from the garden,
I mean to freeze for winter;
Inconsequential things
That made our days . . .

But there is this vast
Uncontrollable silence . . .
Nothing more.

Chapter 24
Making Life Anew

After the first year of being on my own things were beginning to improve a little. Slowly my confidence was returning. Life had to go on. In the meantime the farm would continue. The decison that there was to be no selling out was carried through. The two oldest boys, Richard and Michael had made up their minds they would like to be farmers, manage and work the place between them. Ronnie was still on his world travels. Mahri was married and living in Germany with her soldier husband. Lindsay had left school and was up in Aberdeen working in the oil industry for a core analysis firm, and Kathleen was in her last year at school just dying to leave like the rest of them had been.

I was keen to go fully into writing – perhaps prose as well as poetry if I could find more time. There was one book in particular I wanted to write. I had started it a year or two back at the insistence of a teacher friend. She thought it a good story to tell. I had related to her one day the traumatic time in my life when for three years we had emigrated to the wild prairies of Alberta. The three oldest boys, then all under school age, had gone with us. Mahri and Grant had been born there.

I found it much more difficult to write such a book than to write poetry – the sheer length of it for a start. Besides I got very little encouragement from the literary world I was mixed up in. "Almost impossible," I had been told over and over again, "to get this sort of book published. Unless you are famous in some field or other, no one wants to know about your adventures." I certainly wasn't famous but then neither had Gerald Durell been when he wrote *My Family and Other Animals*, or James Herriot when his vet books first came out.

Progress however was slow. I was easily put off and life kept taking over. I had resolved, however, that I didn't want to take on any permanent farming jobs, like the bookeeping, as so many farmers' wives did and got stuck with. I was not much use at that type of thing anyway and it is time-consuming. This was where Michael's business training came in handy. He said he would take on that job with Richard's assistance. I helped out as usual with taking phone calls, entertaining salesmen, running messages in the busy times, and mediating when there came the inevitable disagreement between the brothers.

A new policy had to be thought out. With Ronald's ill-health over several years and his pessimism about farming the place had become a bit run down. Change was needed – a new policy that would please both the boys. Around that time there were EEC grants going to help farms in like predicaments. The man in charge came out to see us. Between the four of us a policy was worked out. Low cost farming the boys decided was what they would go for. Something they could work between them. The cattle would go altogether and the growing of hay also. We would be purely arable. For this to be viable we were desperately in need of a new barn –somewhere to store grain and potatoes.

The old low stables and cattle sheds that I had looked out on for so long, with their red sandstone walls and pantiled roofs, would have to go. This was a great sadness to me but I couldn't keep back progress. Where would the summer swallows go, who year after year I had watched collecting beakfuls of mud from puddles to repair old haunts or build new nests? Where would they go now?

Actually when the huge new shed did go up I recognised it did have an airy grace with its enormous silver roof reflecting light and the swallows flitted there instead. The new barn was an expensive item. We had it specially insulated for the storage of the potatoes we had decided to grow (our one big mistake as it turned out later).

As well as a new barn we desperately needed a decent drier for the grain and new handling equipment – a new combine – there was so much. There were also forty acres of land that desperately needed draining. A ten year plan was made out. Even with help from the EEC it was going to cost a fortune. Would the farm be able to afford it? We would have to borrow a substantial amount of money. With the see-no-problem attitude of youth and the borrow mentality of the times the boys were fired with enthusiasm. I went along with some trepidation knowing the new ways had to come. The young ones had to do it their way.

Although I still suffered from a kind of that's-life-over feeling, life was beginning to take on a pattern again.

The raspberries were to go. Too many people were now growing them in the district and it was harder and harder to get pickers. Although for seven years we had no disease whatever among the raspberries even although no preventative sprays had been used, this year, partly due to inclement weather, they had mildew. Most of all, however, the reason for giving them up was that the boys didn't like them especially the winter time job of cutting out the old canes and tying up the new – monotonous and time-consuming they said – not worth the trouble.

Although I still suffered from a kind of that's-life-over feeling, my days were beginning to take on a pattern again. Then something happened that took me completely by surprise.

When we were in Canada all those years ago in order to get enough money to live on when we lived in Edmonton, we had taken in a lodger. I had advertised for one in the local papers and was delighted when I heard a Scottish voice over the phone. "Is the room still to let?" Yes it was and so Henry came into our lives. We had all helped one another in those days. Henry was very helpful to us as struggling immigrants. Ronald and he became great friends and for me he became the brother I never had – reliable as daylight. He had come back to Scotland to live much the same time as we did. He wanted to start up in business and Ronald had suggested he come and work at Inchmichael. For various reasons it hadn't worked and he left to work up at Loch Awe in Argyll. Eventually he had started up a business of his own near Linlithgow. Henry had come to visit us from time to time – sometimes at New Year. We all enjoyed those visits –

he never changed. The kids all liked him. They were short on uncles and to them he seemed like a good-humoured generous uncle. He always took them for crisps or sweets – he stayed for a meal and was gone. He was shocked to hear of Ronald's death – came to the funeral – asked if there was anything he could do – and said, "Just get in touch with me if there is."

We saw Henry once or twice that year.

"Just looked in to see how you were getting on."

It was always good to see him. Nice too to talk about Ronald and the time we had in Canada. I seemed to have no one left to talk about old times. The boys always liked Henry's visits – they went up to the pub together.

The following year Henry came first footing. The talk got up about a visit to Edinburgh I was to embark on shortly. Tessa Ransford, president of the Poetry Library, had asked me along to read with Edwin Morgan. I was nervous of driving as far as Edinburgh.

"I'll take you, Mum," Michael had said.

But then Henry had offered. "It won't be any bother," he said, and so it was arranged. I thought it very kind of Henry but then I knew he was a kind man. I didn't really think any further than this until on the way to Edinburgh he withdrew with one hand from the pocket of the car a beautiful box of chocolates and put it on my lap. Then it began to dawn that this was perhaps a little more than just friendship. I didn't know what to say. I was touched. He left me in Edinburgh. I was to stay that night with Tessa and come back by bus. I felt mean about leaving him there but I didn't think he would be interested in a poetry reading.

After that Henry's visits became a bit more frequent. There was a little country pub over the hill where there was dancing on a Saturday night. Would I like to go? I was beginning to feel alive again – life could be fun but I still didn't expect what happened next.

Chapter 25
A Wedding

It was Spring again. This year the sun seemed to shine a little brighter than it had done last year, the first Spring after Ronald died. Had it been sunny at all? I had barely noticed. The sound of the oystercatchers, back from the shore, rang across the green wheat fields. The boys had done a good job with implements that had seen better days and the vibrant green wheat was already looking luxurious on the fertile Carse land.

Nearer at hand the daffodils were out in full glory in the orchard bordering the short drive with its oaks showing as yet no sign of Spring. Each flower was a little sun in itself. The plum trees in the orchard, sadly neglected of late and badly in need of a prune, were a wonderful mass of white blossom. I never tired of looking out at them all the purer and whiter because there was no sign of green leaves yet. Even by moonlight they were beautiful and seemed to shine in the dark with a mysterious essence like the moon itself. The magnolia, its unpruned branches knocking at the sitting room window, was unfolding her exotic white flower like the sails of a yacht or the satin wings of an exotic bird. Perhaps the searing cold winds would not come this year and burn the edges brown. These delicate tender flowers did not belong in this northern climate.

Henry had just paid a short visit and had gone up to the pub with the boys for a pint before returning to Linlithgow. It was a busy time of year for him. I lit the fire in the sitting room. The evening chill was creeping in. The old oaken furniture, the velvet curtains rather faded with age, glowed in the last of the evening sun. I had changed nothing in the sitting room since Ronald had died, wanting it to remain the same. I had just settled down by the blazing flames and had reached for a book when the handle turned in the door. It was Henry.

"I thought you were away."

"I was but I've plucked up courage and come back. I want to ask you something," he answered. "Will you marry me?"

I don't know why I was so completely taken by surprise but I was. Perhaps because remarriage was far from my thoughts. It was just not on my agenda. Who would want a widow with seven kids? Even although they were all growing up now, making their way in the world, who would want me and all my problems?

Henry went on to give some explanation of his sudden proposal.

"I've always cared for you, Margaret, ever since I came to live as your lodger all those years ago in Canada, and I always felt that you cared for me a bit. I admired how you managed to cope in those difficult immigrant years, how you went so cheerfully into hospital to have Grant, how you seldom complained. 'That's the kind of wife I would like,' I said to myself, and in a strange way I thought I might have you for my own one day. But you were happy with Ronald. I would do nothing to disrupt that. Maybe it's just as well, just the same, that my business at Inchmichael, when I returned from Canada, didn't go according to plan and that I left. But you're free now and I could be of help to you."

Honourable as always, I thought, when he fell silent.

"Will you marry me?" he asked again.

Henry did not get the answer he wanted immediately. I had a lot of thinking to do. Was it fair to him – was it fair to the children? I couldn't leave them – not yet – they would need my help for some time to come. Kathleen was still at home – the others making unexpected flurries home – still rolling stones wandering around the world.

"I wouldn't expect you to leave," said Henry. "I could shift my business here – work from here – wouldn't be difficult and I would be on the spot to help you." And I knew he would. Henry had never been anything else but helpful ever since I had first known him.

I thought about it a lot in the next few weeks. I realised how much I cared for him and looked forward to his visits. After being away shopping or attending some writers' meeting, when I turned the corner into the farmyard, would his car be there? There was always disappointment when it wasn't – a sense of excitement and happiness when it was. What would Ronald have thought? But I knew the answer to that one. We had discussed it once or twice. He had said,"If anything should happen to me, Margaret, I wouldn't want you to be unhappy. I would hope you would marry again if you met the right person and that's what you wanted. It wouldn't alter the relationship we have had at all." We had a reciprocal agreement on this.

I knew he would approve of Henry. He'd often said he was his best friend even although he didn't see him often. "He's just so downright straight and honest," he would say. I knew he would not altogether have approved if I had chosen to marry some poet or other. He was always a bit wary of poets – 'unreliable – living in cloud cuckoo land,' he would say.

I confided in the young folk. How would they react? Not one of them said anything other than "that's fine by me, if that's what you want." Fortunately they all liked Henry. "You would let me marry who I want, so of course you can marry who you want," said Michael.

I thought everything through. Marriage is a risk – any marriage at any age is a risk. No one can ever be quite sure how it will work. But I was a good risk taker and it was a risk worth taking.

I was ready with my answer when he returned.

"Better postpone marriage to the end of the year just the same," I said, "to let everyone get used to the idea." Besides, I'd promised to go and stay with Mahri and David in Germany for three weeks in June. "I want to go – want to see if Mahri is managing okay – see if she's feeding herself properly – away out there amongst a lot of strangers."

Events however took over and I realised it would be more expedient to get married sooner rather than later. Our good minister was most helpful and accommodating. "July, well I'm supposed to be on holiday then but I'm not going away anywhere, so I'll be delighted to marry you both." A date was arranged. That gave me two weeks after coming back from Germany to get ready for the wedding. I sent out the invitations before I left. We had decided on the same kind of wedding that

Mahri had. First in the wee church at the foot of the hills and afterwards at Inchmichael.

The three weeks in Germany was a kind of out-of-time experience. David and Mahri were living along with the other soldiers and their wives in a pretty little village called Reinan between Ham and Werl. It had a deer forest coming down into the middle of it. It was clean, neat, picturesque. I was enchanted also by the small towns I saw, often rebuilt in the old style, after massive bombing. The other girls, Mahri's compatriots, welcomed me with open arms. It was a funny set up.

The men folk were often away on exercise. There were no older women for the girls to talk to – no grannies for the children. The older women round about were German and there was the language barrier. An army welfare officer looked after them all – solved problems but it wasn't the same as a mother. For that short time I became a mother to many. I had taken Kathleen with me. She had just left school for good. Katy adored every minute of it especially the outside recreational park where there was a swimming pool with great flumes. First time I had ever seen them. Katy went down these flumes so often in the perpetual sunlight that she was all bruised by the time she got home.

Before we left we had arranged that Mahri should come home for the wedding. When I got back I had two weeks to get ready. I had arranged to have caterers in but there still seemed a great deal to do. By the day of the wedding I was fairly exhausted. The day of the wedding – the last detail seen to – still an hour to go – I lay for a short while in the dappled shade of the leafy orchard with the hard green apples still clinging to the trees. A willow warbler was singing its sad sweet song in the branches above. It was a lovely day. We had been lucky.

And a lovely day it turned out to be. The sun shone for us. No one could have had a happier wedding. Afterwards we were off on a fortnight honeymoon – up north – exploring parts of Scotland that neither of us knew too well – the far north and Orkney. The first of many adventures we were to have together.

Chapter 26
Lindberg's Landing

After the occasion of Mahri's wedding and the big freeze in Scotland were over, Grant had flown back to Canada. He flew to Vancouver this time, thinking that it might be easier to get work on the milder west coast in the winter months. He got a job in Prince Rupert, north of Vancouver, logging for a time but that soon petered out. One evening, in the place that Grant was lodging, he met up with a young fellow much the same age as himself.

"Hi," he said by way of greeting, "how are you?

"So where you from?" came the reply.

Grant was surprised to hear a Scottish voice – a Glasgow accent. They introduced themselves and talked about Scotland for a while. The young man's name was Roy. Eventually they got round to discussing life in Prince Rupert. Roy was also experiencing the same shortage of work.

"What you gonna do?" Roy asked Grant

"I was thinking of hitch hiking to Woking in Alberta where I was before. I've got a van there. I was aimin to fix it up and bring it back here to live in. It would save the expense of lodgings."

"I'll come with you if you like. I was thinkin of goin up north anyway sooner or later. There'll be work there once the big freeze ends," said Roy

"Sure thing," said Grant happy to have a companion from Scotland.

They set off early one morning. It was a long and difficult journey at that time of year – a thousand miles or so to the other side of the Rockies where it would be very cold. Gradually they moved north east with a lift here and a lift there. Grant had a bit of money left. Roy had none at all. Grant bought the food but Roy contributed to their precarious existence by providing, more often than not, the night shelter. Roy was born and brought in Glasgow and was streetwise – knew all the angles. In one small place they landed in, he rang the Salvation Army. They came to collect them and gave them shelter for the night. Sleeping out in the open might mean getting serious frostbite or worse, death from hypothermia. Canadians look after the young no matter how foolish they might think them for the thoughtless journeys they take. At one place a Friendship Society was approached, a charity group run by the Indians. Roy would have asked the Mounties too had he been stuck for somewhere to sleep and had they been in the vicinity. Perhaps they would offer a police cell for the night. Once only did they fail to get anywhere to stay and had to dig into the snow to keep themselves from frostbite.

"Not going to do that again," said Roy in the morning stamping his feet to try and get life back into them.

Eventually they reached Dawson Creek to find it was very cold there indeed.

"I think I'll hitch it back to the west, even if I don't get my van going," Grant said.

Roy was determined to carry on up north.

"Too early," said Grant.

Grant got a hitch to Woking and Roy went further on to Spirit River. They promised to meet up in a couple of days in the café at Spirit River. Grant found when he got to Woking that it was impossible to work on his van in these temperatures. He spent a couple of nights in the trailer home of a friend he had made in his plumbing days, while Roy found his usual accommodation. Two days later they met up as agreed.

"I'm going back to Prince Rupert." Grant was sticking to his plan.

"I'm going further north," said Roy, "there'll be work there soon. Come on Grant, come with me."

Grant was reluctant to do so because of the cold.

"Oh come on, Grant. We'll get a hitch sooner or later." Grant was persuaded.

At Spirit River they stood at the junction for quite some time but eventually were lucky enough to get a lift in a truck to Hay River hundreds of miles away. It was late when they arrived in

Hay River and it had been a long journey. They stayed with the truck driver that night. Next day they had a look round but there didn't seem to be much in the way of work to be had. They had a look at the southern end of the Great Slave Lake. It was still completely frozen over. Someone told them that they should travel to the northern end of the Great Slave – to Yellowknife about a hundred miles away. There would be work there sooner or later and there was good night accommodation in a church. They set off in the late afternoon and began hitching. A few trucks passed them and then a big truck, hauling a boat on a trailer pulled up. The truck window rolled down.

"Where are you guys heading for?" said a Canadian voice.

"Up north," said Roy. "Yellow knife."

"Well I'm sure going in that direction for a bit. Like a lift?" he said.

"Sure," said Roy without hesitation. They jumped into the cab beside the stranger.

"I'm Ed," he introduced himself. "Ed Lindberg."

"I'm Roy," said the Glaswegian, "and this is my buddy Grant. We're both from Scotland looking for work."

"What sort of work?"

"I'm a mechanic," said Roy without hesitation.

"I sure could use a mechanic. In fact I could probably employ both of you. Like to come back to my place?"

Where's your place?" asked Roy.

"Further north," said Ed, "on the banks of the Liard River. The area's called the Blackstone.

"Sure," said Roy. "Why not?"

At the first small township they came to Roy suggested they stop at the beer parlour and have a beer to seal the deal.

"Good idea," said Ed pulling into an almost deserted car lot.

Roy ordered up a round and was asked by the barman for the money.

"You'll have to pay, Ed," he said. "I don't have any."

Being of a generous nature Ed said nothing and reached for his wallet but Grant was quicker and paid for the round. At a later date, remembering the incident, Ed laughed and told me, that at the time, he had thought it a bit rich of Roy asking him to pay for the round especially as he'd given him and his buddy a lift and offered them a job and the drink had been at Roy's invitation. Did I detect a twinkle in Ed's eye – a sneaking admiration for the cheek of it?

A short while afterwards when they were on their way again Ed said, "I'm sure tired. I've have had a heavy day. Think I'll pull into the next rest area and have a nap."

He did just that and promptly fell into a deep sleep. He was a big man and stretched out, taking up most of the cab seat. He began to thrash about in his sleep. There wasn't much room for the boys. Roy stuck it out but Grant got cramp. He opened the cab door and slipped down onto the snow-covered ground. He had forgotten just how perishing it would be now that night had fallen. A truck was coming towards them on the highway. It stopped when it saw Grant pacing up and down. The driver poked his head out of the window.

"What you doin out in the goddamn cold?"

Grant explained about him and his friend Roy in the truck

"That's Ed Lindberg's truck, ain't it?"

"Yip."

"Well you guys be careful, don't you go bumpin him off or nothin. He's a real good guy, Ed." And with that his huge truck took off.

Five more minutes of pacing and Grant knew he would have to get back into the truck otherwise it wouldn't be long until he got frostbite. He squeezed himself back in – Ed never stirred. He and Roy spent a most uncomfortable night but at least they were reasonably warm. Ed woke up early as fresh as the clear northern light of morning.

They drove most of that day. Grant wondered when they were ever going to come to anywhere at all. It was just trees and more trees – no habitation of any kind that he could see. At last on to the Liard highway still under construction and eventually the Blackstone and Lindberg's Landing – a collection of substantial wooden houses, log cabins and bunkhouses. Grant was to remain there for most of the next four years.

Roy didn't last more than a week or two. They were put up in a warm cabin near to the Lindbergs' house and fed in the

Lindbergs' homely kitchen by Sue, Ed's wife.

"At first she must have been a bit suspicious of us – two complete strangers from a foreign land. I didn't say much. You know me, Mum, but Roy with his easy Glaswegian way of talking soon made everyone relax. Sometimes, in the evening we would play cards. Roy was good at cards and he could get people laughing which always helps. Roy, however, wasn't as good a mechanic as he had confidently asserted himself to be. One day, while tearing a chainsaw to pieces to find out what was wrong, both Ed and I got on to him for his rough handling of it."

"A bunch of old women," he said downing tools. He walked off, packed his rucksack and made for the highway. At the junction where the rough road of Lindberg's Landing met the new Liard highway, Roy came face to face with a huge black bear. As luck would have it a grader came up the road and gave him a lift.

Grant learned a very great deal in his four years at Lindberg's Landing. He did all sorts of jobs. To begin with he helped to build various workshops and cabins. He also helped with the sawmill and to plant potatoes. Sometimes he helped Sue who took on an immense gardening workload not to mention bringing in washing water, feeding and milking goats and chickens. A big area had been cleared from the bush for a garden. Sue showed him examples of the vegetables she had grown the previous year still useable out of the root cellar. He was surprised how well things grew so far north in such a short summer and reckoned it must be because their were so many hours of sunlight. Vegetables were stored in the root cellar, a dark cave deep in the ground which kept the root vegetables from freezing solid. Dry food stuff, flour, coffee etc. was kept in a catche – a small hut on stilts, that was reached by a ladder. They were put there for safety to keep predators such as bears from stealing vital food stuff. Meat was kept frozen in tin boxes and buried in the snow. There was so much to be done just in the name of survival. In return he was well fed on moose and caribou meat, pike from the river, roots from the cellar, bannock which Sue baked on the black stove and provisions brought in, from time to time, from Fort Simpson. Later Ed had work for him taking down trees and sawing up wood. For a while he got a job on the Liard highway. In the making of this road they had much muskeg to overcome, many streams to bridge. The most difficult job of all Grant told me was trying to mix concrete when constructing those bridges in freezing conditions when the push was on to finish the road for a deadline – the road that was eventually to run two hundred miles or more to Fort Nelson.

"We were waiting for Grant and the squad to finish the Liard highway," was Ed's grandiose way of putting it. Ed may have exaggerated what Grant achieved but it made up for Grant always belittling his own work.

Ed got contracts from time to time and employed Grant to help. Grant was now making dollars and there was little to spend them on. Besides felling timber in the bush and working on the saw mill, Grant learned how to fashion all sorts of things from wood. At one point he helped build a substantial log cabin. All this was to be a great use to him when he came back to Scotland.

"Grant would tackle anything," I was told at a later date by Ed Lindberg. "You just had to tell him what was wanted and he would go out and find a way of doing it."

Thrown in at the deep end of things, having to lay your hand to anything, was a great teacher. This sort of opportunity was so often lacking at home in the modern world.

After a year at Lindberg's Landing Grant, with Ed's guidance, was building himself a boat, large and strong enough to sail down the Liard River to Fort Simpson seventy five miles away. When Lindsay came out the following summer they had the inaugural launch and sail. Lindsay and he very nearly came to grief in a sudden storm where the Mackenzie meets the Liard but managed to limp into the safe haven of Fort Simpson. Neither of them had done any sailing before.

Ed had a boat of his own for general use. For so long the only way to get to anywhere at all had been by boat down the river in summer and by ice road on the river in winter. Ed also had a dredger. There was gold in the Liard River – thin films of it that were difficult to extract from the mud. A way had been found.

"One day I'll get round to it," Ed kept saying.

When the Liard highway came near to completion Ed got

the contract to construct the Blackstone Park. A surveyor was sent to lay it out. She was a woman and had problems with the clouds of mosquitoes, the threat of the ever present bears, and the thickness of the bush. Grant was sent to help her fix up the yellow ribbons. Later he got the job of clearing the forty bays marked out that would be used for visiting campervans etc or RV's as they are called (recreational vehicles). He was praised for his work. He was also given the job of constructing the picnic tables and helping with the loos etc. Because he had done so well in clearing the bush for the Blackstone Park he was asked, some time later, to take on the much larger job of felling trees in a big area of bush near Fort Simpson. The Pope was paying a visit to Fort Simpson while on crusade in Canada.

"Why Fort Simpson?" I asked Grant

"Dunno really. Perhaps they just stuck a pin on a map of the North West Territories with their eyes closed and chose where it landed.

They needed to clear an area of bush to allow the First Nation people, as the Indians are now called, to congregate – different tribes coming from from far and wide – somewhere to put up their tents.

This project happened to come up in the same summer that Lindsay was at the Lindbergs'. Grant and he and a crew of fifteen First Nation men set out to tackle the job. They started work at 7am. Lindsay and Grant were felling sizeable trees with power saws. Lindsay had never done this in his life before – had to have quick reactions when a tree fell in the opposite direction to the one he had anticipated. At one point Grant put his power saw further in to the trunk of a tree than he should have done and it stuck with the tree on the point of falling. If this happened safety instructions are to leave the saw and scarper. Grant was determined to release the saw and did so but had to take a tremendous leap at the last moment as the tree came crashing down. The saw was undamaged. Fortunately I didn't hear, until much later, about all the dangerous situations they got themselves into. By 11am the fifteen First Nation men knew it was an impossible task they had been given. The boss came round to see how they were getting on and they demanded more money. They didn't get it so took what they had earned that morning and went to the beer parlour. For a while Grant and Lindsay carried on. One of the First Nation men hadn't left with the others. He was an older man who sat under a tree and sharpened the saws for the boys. Sitting still with his back straight, Grant said he looked like a figure carved out of stone. The next time the boss came round he realised it was an impossible job he had given the boys to do in the time allotted and got the bulldozers in.

On the day the Pope was due to arrive a thick mist hung low over Fort Simpson. Planes couldn't land. The Pope didn't see Fort Simpson at that time, but journeyed there two years later.

One winter Grant spent a week on the trapline with one of Ed's helpers called John. They visited all the traps on the line sleeping at nights in a tent warmed by an airtight wood stove. Not so long ago this had been the only way of making a living – surviving in these far north places. Trappers lived by the money they got for the furs of martin and lynx – the moose and caribou they shot to eat. In winter the traps were visited on a regular bases and the captured animals removed. Usually they were dead and frozen solid. Only the lynx with its remarkable coat might survive. In the last trap they came to, on that particular excursion, there was a live lynx – a beautiful creature. Grant would have liked to have let it go but couldn't without it tearing him to pieces. Grant didn't seek to go on the trap line again – didn't like this way of making a living but knew, that not so long ago, it was a necessary in order to live there. Life was tough in these northern lands and you had to be tough to survive.

Many interesting people passed through Lindberg's Landing. I listened endlessly to the tales brought home by Grant and Lindsay. Many visitors came to see the Lindbergs – adventurous people who had sailed up the Liard in summer. In hundreds of miles there were few stopping places. No one would bypass the Lindbergs'. Ed's father, Ole Lindberg, had been there before him and was now a legend. Ed and Sue entertained them all. Then there were the daring bush pilots who looked in, from time to time, and men looking for logs. The summer that Lindsay was there, three huge men came from Norman Wells looking for logs to build houses.

"Having worked in the woods a lot they had six fingers between them," Lindsay told me, "and they smoked tobacco that was so strong we couldn't go near them without spluttering and choking."

They got the logs they wanted, bored holes at the ends and lashed them tightly together into a raft. It had to be strong enough to take them down the Liard River that flowed north east to the Beaufort Sea in the Arctic Circle. Six hundred miles or so they had to sail down to Norman Wells negotiating, in places, beaver dams and rapids. On this raft they tied down a tent and sailed off one sunny day. What a picture on the mind this story of the boys gave to me. These big men sailing away on this tremendous raft smoking the strongest of strong cigarettes. To add to the picture one of them owned a brightly coloured parrot which sat on his shoulder wherever he went.

There were other interesting people who passed through. People from all walks of life interested in the adjacent Nahanni district. Up till recently this had been an almost inaccessible spot. It was now of world wide scientific and geological interest. There is still no road to it except for the ice road in winter. In the summer you travel there by plane or boat. It has high mountains, the Mackenzie range, lakes, rivers and somewhere, hidden in the hinterland, a waterfall that is reputed to be twice the height of the Niagara Falls. Its hazards are remorseless fierce frost in winter, clouds of mosquitoes for much of the summer and the ubiquitous bear.

Lindberg's Landing looked over to the Mackenzie mountains and Nahanni Bute one of its highest peaks. It was from Lindberg's Landing that Grant brought back the skills that were to lead to diversification on the farm of East Inchmichael.

Chapter 27
Summer Wine

Given that the Gillies children were all to some degree travellers, not all them were present at the wedding of Henry and I. Grant was still in the North West Territories, in Canada.

Ronnie, in a gap in his world travels did attend with his new girlfriend. It was some time since he had been home. He had gone to Australia on a year's work permit with the intention of finding a job and perhaps staying on, but circumstances were against him. Nowadays he was running out of companions to go abroad with for long spells. His friends and contemporaries were beginning to settle down.

He had many adventures in Australia – got a job here and there, but decided he would like to see as much of the country as he could and went on a 5,000 mile hitch hike. The size of the place fascinated him – so much of it red desert. You could travel for days and days over arid red desert and the landscape didn't change much. The deeper he got into the bush the more difficult it became to get lifts but he persevered. In one small place he landed in he was stuck for several days. Eventually he begged some aborigines to take him to the next place. They were none too keen but agreed. The most uncomfortable bumpy slow ride he had had in his whole life but he was grateful to them just he same.

They took him to Halls Creek and in this most unlikely of all places he found work. A party of geologists were eager to take him on. Not that Ronnie knew anything of their trade but they needed a cook a handyman – some one that could turn his hand to anything. Ronnie was a master at that. Sometimes they even had him do some measuring. Ronnie wondered why they bothered measuring land that went on for ever and seemed so similar.

144

One day after measuring out a piece of land one of the geologists said, "Now name it." Ronnie had built a small cairn in the middle of the red rock. "Oh," he said, "how about Cairn – no – Mohr? Kind of Gaelic," he said. Mohr means big.

Mostly he was cooking though. Ronald was happy here. He got on well with the geologists and he got well paid. A helicopter kept them in touch with Perth, Australia. He might have remained with them but circumstance took over. Fire. Fires broke out from time to time in Australia – a natural process of burn and regrowth. This was a particularly bad one. The flames were coming at their tiny encampment from all angles at an unprecedented rate.

"Never have I felt so vulnerable, Mum," said Ronnie, after returning home. "Here we all were, standing in our miniature quadrangle fashioned from the bush, holding what seemed to be tiny pails of water. Then the wind changed. Had it not I think we would have all been burnt to a frazzle. The team lost most of their equipment."

I thought perhaps Ronnie would settle after his Australian jaunt. Not Ronnie. As soon as he had saved enough again he was off. With some students this time and another old jalopy to see as much of Europe as they could in the long student holidays. They were mostly boys, but there was one pretty girl with them – a medical student called Judith. I had seen her once when she visited the bothy to see what she could do to help a fellow student who had broken a leg. She looked very young, had a sweet smile but seemed extremely competent. In the north of Italy the car eventually broke down, or rather the brakes gave out. In the small town they were in, the parts were not in stock. They would have to wait.

The other students drifted off home hitch hiking where they could. Judith stayed with Ronnie – a whole fortnight they waited in this beautiful place beside a lake. After Ronnie got home Judith became his steady. Perhaps Ronnie would think of settling down now, think of something to do – he wanted to have a business of his own. He was always coming up with new ideas some of them most impractical. He started to make clocks out of rounds of wood using the natural grain on them to make faces. They were attractive. Ronnie was artistic and always saw unusual possibilities in things. They did sell but I couldn't see how he could sell enough to make a real living. Judith, in any spare moments, away from her studies, helped him all she could.

Then they started to make wine in fairly large quantities. The farmhouse kitchen was the ideal place. They experimented with different fruits and leaves. Their friends lapped it up. Ronald and Judith were a popular couple – too popular. Perhaps they could do this commercially. I was dubious myself, what with reputed wine lakes in Europe.

> "I believed always in encouragement – you just never knew what might take off."

"This will be different, Mum," Ronnie explained his enthusiasm alight. "We want to get away from the highbrow image of wine – this wine will be fun, good and made from local fruits and plants."

I believed always in encouragement. You just never knew what might take off. I had five years of wine in the kitchen, sticky floors and bubbling demi-johns all around. Beautiful colours they were – the deep champagne of strawberry or the wonderful clear ruby red of bramble, and the deeper hues of elderflower.

I rather liked my new music from the bubbling demi-johns, an accompaniment to the poems I wrote when I got up in the middle of the night. The boot cupboard became a store. It was usually overflowing. "I wonder if I will always remember these early days," said Judith, "of trying to squeeze one more demi-john of wine into the boot cupboard."

I was pleased about Ronnie's new girlfriend. Perhaps he will settle down, I thought. But the following year they were off again. Judith had decided to take a year out at a hospital in India. Ronnie went with her.

Chapter 28

Coming Home to Roost

Marriage to Henry made a huge difference to my life. It was hard at first to get into the new routine. Some one was doing something for me. Not that my family had not been considerate in the past, but it's just that growing up is difficult. It needs help and backing from an older generation. It's difficult also to change. Here I was still putting sugar in their tea. Sometimes in moments of thoughtlessness I would put sugar in strangers' teas. I had just got so used to doing things for people. Now Henry was doing things for me – looking after me as well as getting on with his own welding business. He was also helping the boys on the farm, lending a hand at busy times, or mending up implements, a most necessary contribution that saved them a lot of money.

It wasn't that he said much. He wasn't a man of many words. It was more what he did – tended the garden, took responsibilities off my back whenever he saw the opportunity, encouraged me to continue with my writing especially the book about our years in Canada.

Sometimes, looking back I had thought the Canada episode had had little impact on our lives but I was wrong. For a start I would not have met Henry. He would not have been a welder with a business of his own. Our farming policy might have been different. I might not have become quite so self-reliant and unconcerned as to what others thought. Grant would not be in Canada now. My children might not have developed this insatiable wanderlust. I would not have this deep desire to write this book about our Canadian experience against all odds.

One day, not too long after we were married, Henry bought me one of the early Amstrad computers. He got advice from one of his brothers-in-law who knew about these things. I had been struggling away with an old typewriter, typing and re-typing.

I wasn't good at it. It would take me for ever. Now I had this computer which did marvellous things. However to begin with it was very difficult. Not many people had them at the time. How would I ever learn? The manual that came with them seemed very complicated. There were a few classes but I thought they might have confused me even further. The easiest way would have been to learn step by slow step with the aid of some kind person who knew what they were doing. But there were very few. Brother-in-law Tom helped me a lot and his daughter Carol. And then Brenda, my university friend, got one and we did a lot of working out together. However in the beginning, had it not been a present from Henry and because I was determined it would be of use, it might have gone crashing through the window in sheer exasperation. Once I learned the rudiments, it became the most valuable thing I possessed.

I finished my manuscript and got it up on the screen. Once there I could make any improvements I wished so easily, it was a joy. Initially I printed out two copies – one to keep for myself – one to send out. I got hold of the Writers and Artists Yearbook and sent it to whoever I thought the most likely taker. Months would go by and six months later it would come back with little comment other than "although an interesting story we are not really interested in anything autobiographical unless you are famous".

So all my doubting literary advisers had been right. However I wasn't going to be put off that easily but I did reckon that if I sent it out to a lot of publishers, it could take forever, especially if they all took six months to return the book. Some warned me about a year's delay before it was sent back. I decided to print out five chapters selected from the book and write a synopsis and send five or six out at a time. Sooner or later they all came bounding back mostly with the same story. Fictionalise it, some said. One or two were kind enough to praise it. Hodder & Stoughton said it was like a breath of fresh air coming into their stuffy London office – they enjoyed it, but no. I think it was those one or two that had praised it, genuinely, that kept me going. After the manuscript came back thirty times I re-read it myself and decided it wasn't well enough written.

I then did two things. One, I asked a few literary friends whose opinion I respected if they would be so kind as to read it and give me an honest assessment. Two, I started to write a romance for a Mills & Boon type market. I had to learn how to write a story and figured the only real way to gain experience was to do it.

We had a good summer that year. I can remember how much I enjoyed sitting out writing in glorious sunshine in the quiet garden that Henry was getting into some sort of shape after years of neglect. I was thoroughly enjoying writing a romance. Each Tuesday I went into the Dundee University group with the next instalment. They all seemed to enjoy it – couldn't wait for the next, they said – quite a few laughs also with my poor heroine Becky and the nasty Penelope Fox-Pitt, the rude-to-begin-with hero, all genre material.

I sent it to Mills & Boon and they turned it down. To be quite honest I think it was a bit tongue in cheek which they don't like and there was no explicit sex which they were now beginning to go into. I sent it to Robert Hale. "Send in back in six months," they said, "we are snowed under with mss. just now but we will consider it later." However when I did send it back they said they were reorganising what they published and had discontinued this line.

My world outside literature was still very busy. Different in some ways but busy. Sometimes there were none of the younger members of the family at home. Michael now had a cottage of his own on the farm. Lindsay was more or less living up in Aberdeen or away on world adventures like the rest. Kathleen, after a year at home once she left school, had also gone to Aberdeen to live.

The old farm house wasn't bulging at the seams any more. Well not all the time, but visitors would appear out of nowhere – there was always room for them. Sometimes I would be going back upstairs in the mornings to make the beds and meet someone coming down I had never seen before.

"Sorry Mum, forgot to tell you. She's a pal I met in Australia." or "Sorry Mum. He's from Baghdad. He was hitch hiking. It was absolutely coming down in buckets. We gave him a lift. Awful late to go to a youth hostel so we brought him here."

Sometimes, however I was asked.

"A friend I met in India. Do you think you could put him up for a week or so."

"Tell me something about him."

"Well he's Indian."

"Uh huh."

"And he's a priest."

"Oh."

"He helped Judith and I a lot when we were in India. He was kind to us. After Judith finished her doctoring we wanted to do some work on the land. No one needs you to work on the land in India – they've got plenty workers but Dharma Raj took us in, fed us, kept us, got us small jobs to do. I owe him. He's quite a man, Mum. You'll like him."

Prepared to a certain extent I was still unprepared for the phone call and a sing-songy Indian voice asking for Ronnie. Ronnie was off on one of his jaunts. Who was he speaking to? For a moment I couldn't think. Mum, I said. He called me mum from then on. I wasn't quite prepared either for the small dark man with shining eyes and a cheerful expression dressed in a black priest gown and a sparkling white dog collar. Made of plastic, it turned out. Henry and I enjoyed his visit very much. Everything was so new to him. He had never been outside India.

"How different is it?" I asked him one evening.

"Too different," he said. "So much so that I can't even begin to tell you – there are no points of contact." He spoke beautiful English. It was rather a slack time for us on the farm when he arrived. We were thinking he would view us as rather lazy.

"And you people," he said, "you are always working. You do not throw banana skins on the ground, spit or sit on the roads and wail." I thought the latter was highly improbable in Scotland. You would either get soaked, freeze or get run over very quickly.

The day after he came he went to visit the Catholic church in Dundee. The priest there asked him if he would consider taking over his church for a month while he went on holiday – take charge – someone different, the congregation would like it.

"What do you think?" I was surprised he asked me.

"Of course," I said.

150

"I'll have to go to London – get my visa extended." He was a great success in Dundee. Before he left the *Evening Telegraph* ran a feature on him. What were you most surprised at in this country? was one of the questions he was asked.

"Everything is a surprise," he said, "often a delightful surprise. What shocked me most was a choice of food for dogs and cats when so many people, children, go starving in India!"

Darma Raj came back twice to visit us. Sent by his Bishop on church business, hoping to raise money for his orphan boys. He had two hundred under his care. The Indian government would give no money to Christians. Some way or other he had to find it. We raised a fund for him on the farm and gave what we could. Ronnie had been at his place in India and knew he was genuine. Once a year he bought what he called paddy for his boys – rice off the field at harvest time. He used every bit of it. What wasn't used for eating went for fuel for cooking. He grew vegetables with the help of the boys and they kept a few buffalo from which they got milk. It was thick and creamy. They watered it down. There was plenty for everyone. The boys slept on the roof under the stars. It was safer that way. There were still dangerous tigers in the forest. He slept on the roof as well, every night, to look after them. He never got a full night's sleep always there was crying in the night. Some new orphan needing comforting.

The second time he came to visit us he had been in America.

"Fantastic," he told us, they have everything, absolutely everything and they were very kind to me. Wanted me to stay. But I couldn't desert my India, my orphans. They have everything apart from one thing."

"What's that?" I asked.

"Peace of mind," he said. "Oh if I could just bring peace of mind out of my pockets," he said dipping his dark hands into his anorak and bringing them out again empty, "and sell it, oh what a fortune I would make for my orphans."

Ronnie's last time in India was his last lengthy visit to another country. Judith had her exams to finish. She was in her final year and then there would be a year working as a house doctor. The current students had left the bothy that Spring. The bothy would suit Ronnie well to live in.

Not long after that Grant returned from Canada. "I don't think I'll go back. I love it way up north, wouldn't want to be in any other part, but it will never be my country. Ed Lindberg hasn't so much work for me at the moment and I really don't feel like I can stay there and work for others – they are so kind and I can't take advantage of them like that. I've been staying in Fort Simpson lately with Ed's mother – she is a very kind lady but she's getting on a bit now. And it's Indian territory up there, quite rightly so – they've taken everything else away from them. It means however all sorts of problems. I wouldn't be able to buy land outright to build a house or anything like that. Anyway, I want to be home. I miss the kitchen and the family and the farm and company I understand.

"What will you do now?"

"Go and see if there is some course I can get on that will give me some qualifications."

"What?"

He seemed hazy. "Dunno. The Kingsway Tech has an open day next Tuesday. I'll go and see – decide then."

He came back in what I thought was remarkably quick time.

"Already," I said.

"No. I got to the car park. Parked the car and couldn't go inside. I knew I couldn't do it, couldn't speak to strangers. Been in the bush too long."

Henry who was having his lunch asked, "Grant, what would you really like to do?"

"Have a business of my own. Do something in the wood line. I've learned a great deal about it in Canada. Made all sorts of things from log houses to lavatories."

"Why don't you then?"

"Too difficult," said Grant.

Henry rose from the table and disappeared for two or three minutes.

"No it's not," he said when he returned, "all you need is an invoice book and a saw – and he handed him the necessary requirements.

Chapter 29
A House Together Stands

If there was one thing the farm could boast of, it was that it had plenty of unused buildings. Buildings that had become too small for modern day farming or were no longer needed because farming policy had changed. Henry now worked from the old water tank that had once been fed by windmills before mains water had been put in. His workshop turned out all manner of things, but chiefly, when we first got married, huge steel buckets for JCBs.

But Henry was an inventor at heart, always thinking out new things that would be useful to people. He wasn't so fussy about how they looked as to how well they would work, how strong and reliable they were. Eventually buckets were to become unprofitable because of the increased price of the raw material and he went on to other things. One especially good idea he had never got off the ground, even although everyone he had mentioned it to thought it was a winner.

It was a turntable made of steel that a car could drive onto and be very easily turned. But try as we could the idea never caught on. Had we been able to afford a vast advertising campaign perhaps it would have but this Henry was not prepared to do. It would make life too complicated. All he wanted to do was make something serviceable, enjoyable, strong and of a price people could afford. Eventually he hit on something that did all of these things – wood burning stoves. He was kept busy with these especially in winter.

The water tank cum machinery repair shop stood at the back of the house near the old Dutch barn. It had a wonderful outlook to the east across the wide Carse land to the burgeoning city of Dundee twelve miles away on the horizon. Neighbouring farmers, miles away, would remark on Henry's blue flashing welding lights being visible late into the winter evenings when few other lights pierced the bramble blackness. Henry knew what was necessary in business. "You must be able to make something enough people need and at a competitive price. This it was getting more and more difficult to do with mass production but there is always a gap somewhere if you can just find it."

The farm was in a good position from which to sell goods. It stood in the centre of the Carse of Gowrie between two towns – twelve miles from Perth, twelve miles from Dundee, and had the well-populated Fife, Angus and Perthshire on its doorstep. Our local paper was also important. It served them all and its small ads were very reasonably priced.

Grant was given a bit of the old stable for his workshop in front of which stood a long open-fronted cart shed. Once it had held a dozen horses and as many carts and faced onto a large stack yard. There was plenty of room should his business ever expand. Grant loved working in wood, was good at it, and had had a lot of practice in Canada. To begin with he concentrated on small things like garden furniture mostly, chairs, picnic tables, bird tables, anything that there might be a demand for. However, as much as he loved the work he was finding it hard to make ends meet – the profit on each item was low – too many people were doing the same thing and garden centres were becoming so popular and they sold a lot of these things.

However he was kept busy. So much so, that he asked if Ronnie would help. One day he decided he needed a different sort of saw. The *Courier* was advertising what he needed at a reasonable price. He went to get it from a man in Dundee whom he found to be making garden sheds out of old wood.

"Can't make enough of them," he told Grant.

"Why don't you try that then Grant?" I said when he told me and so the first garden shed was made. Off Ronnie and he went in his old car with trailer, improvised by Henry to deliver and erect it. The delighted purchaser gave them a hundred ten pound notes. As soon as they were round the corner they stopped the car, counted out the notes and Whoopee! – they threw the lot up in the air to hit the roof of the car and come fluttering down again – they were in business. And they were. They had hit on something enough people wanted and were willing to pay a reasonable price for. Big superstores sold them but the wood was not of such good quality and people mostly had to erect them themselves. Here service was given and if anyone wasn't satisfied they could be easily contacted and would rectify anything that was wrong.

Judith was now with Ronald in the bothy. For a while she cycled the twelve miles every day into the university. Her first job as house doctor was in Bridge of Earn. On the days she didn't have to stay there overnight she cycled there.

> "The farmers around were amazed at her versatility – 'and a girl too!' "

She was a country girl at heart and fit. She began to realise however, that she didn't really want to be a doctor. This was not the life she wanted. All the silent pressures had kept her going. But she didn't really like it – the hierarchy of doctors – the terrifying possibilities of things going wrong, but most of all, being cloistered for so long in antiseptic corridors. She was an outdoor girl, loved the fresh air and freedom. Besides, she began to see shades of the prison house and how doctoring would begin to dictate her life. It wasn't all that easy to get a job and you had to keep going. Judith decided she would stop for a year and go into the making of sheds to help Ronnie and perhaps, one day they would do something about their wine-making and get a winery started.

So Judith joined the shed-making team and, rather to the boys' surprise, was a great asset. She went out with Ronnie and Grant to erect the buildings. Roofs had to be put on on site and before they could argue Judith was up on the top of sheds as lithe as any squirrel. The farmers around were amazed at her versatility – "and a girl too!" I think Judith must have been brought up, as I was, to believe a girl could do anything if she really wanted to. Her folks were of that persuasion – they had five daughters and a son.

Ronnie and Judith, however really wanted to set up a winery.

They still had wine bubbling away in every available nook and cranny. They needed more space and a bit of money to get what was required. The farm couldn't help with money. We were badly overdrawn with the new improvements but once again we could help with space. On either side of the old brick bothy ran even older and more dilapidated cart sheds. They would need a lot done to them but could be utilised.

All the boys helped – Grant with the plumbing, Richard with the electricity, the farm boys with the building using the lovely old sandstone kept from other demolished buildings. Between them all, it seemed, they knew or learned how to do everything. No outside expensive tradesmen needed to be called in. Ronnie and Judith did a bit of everything. I had often said as my mother had said before me, "a house together stands, divided falls." It was coming true.

Chapter 30

The Banker Cometh

With the family all working together, of course there were quarrels, and wrong turnings. It was by no means plain sailing. Many of the arguments took place in the farm kitchen. Often I stood in as mediator. Being equally interested in all the points of view I could more easily see the overall picture and what was going wrong. Knowing all their diverse characters also, I could point out why each acted the way they did. There was always a good deal of humour around. They could all laugh at each other's foibles and more importantly at their own.

The boys had diverse ways of doing things on the farm. They wanted to grow different crops. Michael was keen to grow potatoes even though we were allowed to grow only ten acres because of government quotas. Having worked with his uncle, Michael knew about potatoes. Not quite enough as it turned out. After several years they almost brought us to disaster. They involved a tremendous amount of work and prevented the other crops being attended to properly. Merchants had the potato world sown up. Few individual farmers grew them these days and instead rented out the land to the merchants who could afford to buy the big potato machines. It was no longer profitable to hire in pickers and planters even supposing you could get them. Gone were the good old days. Now workers had to be bussed in from the cities.

There were times also when too much nitrogen was put on the wheat, not taking in what came from natural sources. At harvest time, if there was much rain the over-heavy crop would go down. A few years of heavy rain sorted that one out. "Experience," someone once said, "is the best teacher, but she is very expensive." We were all finding that out the hard way.

Of course my advice, if taken, could be equally as wrong.

Farming has never been anything other than a gamble and is often worked on hunches. The boys however were gathering praise from round about on how well Inchmichael was looking, how good their crops were.

Having learned from his uncle how to work, Michael had hardly stopped since. The only problem was, if possible, he would have liked to do everything himself. In ploughing, he thought, Richard did not draw a straight enough furrow and missed bits in cultivating. Richard had a much more laid-back attitude to life. "Oh well if Michael wants to do it, let him get on with it," was his way of looking at it.

" 'Experience,' someone once said, 'is the best teacher, but she is very expensive.' "

One winter's day I said to Michael, "Have you seen anything strange down the fields lately?" meaning in the way of wild life.

"Well actually I have Mum," he said, "Richard ploughing."

This was a joke in the family for years, Richard laughing along with the rest. But if Richard had some weaknesses he also had strengths. Michael was not a good bargainer. Salesmen, to begin with, could run rings round him but Richard could hold out until he got a good deal.

In spite of everything, however, a few years into farming by the boys and myself, we came near to the brink of disaster. It was caused by a combination of a run of bad summers, low farming prices, but most of all because we had borrowed too much money. I had tried to warn the boys but this was an age of borrowing. The banks pushed money at you but took no risks themselves and could foreclose if you went over the mark. I knew we were in trouble when I got a phone call one day. It was the banker.

"I'm coming down to see the crops. When would it be suitable?"

"I'll see the boys and ring you back," I said. No banker had been near Inchmichael for years. What do you do? I wondered.

I remembered long ago the tactics of my mother's farming family. You ask the banker down for lunch and give him a good meal and a glass of wine. He was duly invited to come one day in June when the crops were at their most lush and the oil seed rape a brilliant yellow. This new crop had swept over Scotland like yellow fire. Fields everywhere were exploding suns, brightening the day even if the sun was behind a cloud. Early morning walks were heaven those days. The air was fresh and sweet with the honey scent of the rape seed flower. There was always the chance of seeing a rich brown roe deer leaping over the sun-coloured fields. Sometimes her dappled fawns would venture out on to the farm road. They were born in this crop which grew so fast you could almost see it growing. It gave good impenetrable cover where deer were safe to have their young.

Before the banker came I had discussions with everyone. "Now we'll all need to pull together. The other businesses will need to try and help if need be – all electricity must be paid for and the milk bill from the separate households – it always seemed to be too high. Thousands owing, and yet that was the problem – the milk bill! It became a standing joke – whenever there were cash flow problems in the family. "It will be the milk bill!" I did stress at this time to all of the family, the farm is the golden egg from which our lives comes. We must take care of it.

I excelled myself with the meal for the banker. Extra special soup. I still always had a huge pot of it on the hob for all the hungry people that strayed into the kitchen at lunch time but I added even more flavours and cream. Then I had sea trout freshly caught from the Tay with salad and a Hungarian recipe, chicken oregano, that I had got from a friend in Canada. Fluffy jellies and the first of the season's strawberries to finish. Then of course there was wine – Ronnie's wine – the bramble, a glorious clear red the colour of sparkling rubies and Springoak the palest gold.

I brought out my best Madeira embroidered cloth, and set the table in the chapel. It was either there or the kitchen. We had no dining room these days.

In the end I need not have gone to so much trouble. He turned out to be one of the nicest bankers I have ever met and as far as we were concerned the right man at the right time – a saviour.

He was taken a tour of the farm by the boys. It was a lovely June day of sparkling sunshine – the farm looked well. Afterwards, over a pre-lunch glass of wine he got into conversation with us all. He was a father figure of a man and treated the boys more as sons than clients. It was obvious he was disillusioned by the modern systems of banking himself.

"That's the way it is nowadays," he said not being able to hide a little bitterness in his voice. "Nothing is sacred. Money is the God. Sentiment of any kind is out the window. These cottages you own could bring in a lot of money one way or another. You could sell them or get a good rent. Each one should pay its way." I thought of Sissy, the widow of one of our ploughmen. It would kill her to ask her to leave her home. Besides she was almost a second mother to the family. And the last of the students and Ronnie in the bothy rent-free while he tried to get his business going – no way.

We would find some other way – not that.

"It is possible for you to get out of this debt but it will take a long time. What you must do is keep forward books. Notice carefully what you are doing and spending," said the banker.

I was actually more optimistic than he was. We had begun to rectify some of the mistakes and we had come through four bad years weatherwise – surely it would be a good one this year. That was always the way of farming and always would be. Besides we had decided to give up potatoes. They were losing us money. And this newish crop that I thought so beautiful while it was in flower – oil seed rape. It was doing well. How about linseed? It was in vogue this year. I had seen a field of it once in flower. I had thought it a loch I had not realised was there. It was the colour of blue water. How lovely it would look next to a field of rape – they both flowered at the same time. Actually the boys did try it at a later date, half to please me. It was as beautiful as I thought it would be. I took photographs. But it was the worst crop we ever grew. Impossible to harvest because of its tough stalks and lateness in ripening. We never grew it again. "Mum, you and your beautiful crops."

I had to admit I wasn't really a very good farmer – far too impractical and I did things for wrong reasons. The boys were much better at it than me and they were learning – never more than that day with the banker.

The meal afterwards was pleasant indeed. The banker told us a little about himself. He came of farming people – understood farming and farmers. His heart lay there. He didn't really like this bank in Perth. It was too big and had too many clients who weren't farmers. He didn't like the modern way of doing things. He actually remained in the Perth branch only for a further year. I expect he asked to be moved to smaller town – a farming town.

In the middle of the meal the phone rang. It was for Michael.

"Sorry everyone I've got to go," he said. Apart from the banker we all knew why he had to go. Michael by this time had a partner Denise, whom he hadn't mentioned to the banker. It was hard explaining to a different generation. The phone call was from the hospital. Michael's first child was about to be born. We got a phone call a few hours later.

"Mother, I've got a son."

Chapter 31
Expanding Family

While Grant had gone off again travelling for a while, Ronald and Judith had built up a good business in the shed line. They called their business Natty Sheds. On his return, Grant decided to continue the shed business but he needed a partner. He had a friend in Errol called John Mackay who was a landscape gardener. They became partners. At first they did a bit of landscaping as well as building sheds and renamed the business Garden Craft as this would cover all eventualities However they found the making of sheds more profitable than the landscaping and concentrated on that. They moved into making other things – anything from rabbit hutches to solar cabins – bird houses to summerhouses – wendy houses, stables – anything. Gradually the name Garden Craft was dropped and they became Gillies and Mackay.

Grant loved working in wood. John was catching up fast and he brought other skills to the business. He was good at talking to customers – the business side of things. The business kept growing. From one small weekly ad in the *Courier*, the local paper with a wide distribution, they got plenty of orders. Grant fulfilled a wish of his by building a log cabin with the complete logs, a replica of one he had built in the bush in Canada. It served as their office.

In the busy season they were beginning to have too much to do. From March till October we could hear hammering far into the night. They employed more lads from the village. One of the things I admired about the business was the harmony in the workshop. Grant and John were fair to everyone they employed— when the business did well, everyone did well. But as in any business it wasn't all plain sailing. Things went wrong from time to time. It was very competitive – the price had to be right and there was no great profit in any one thing. The proper wood had to be bought – the best at the cheapest price. For quite a while wood that came from Russia was often the best value. "There can't be over much sentiment in business," they would tell me.

One year they came near to disaster. It was one of Scotland's unusually dry and sunny summers. The sheds were made in the usual way but the wood shrunk with the extreme dryness leaving gaps here and there. That year they had to replace forty sheds. From that experience, of course, they learned to make sheds in a different way so that it wouldn't happen again.

To begin with I helped out a bit taking phone calls etc, but soon it was decided they needed a secretary. John's 'other half', Caroline, offered to help out when she could. I thought this very noble of her as they had a young family of five children. But help she certainly did and she was good at her job. Quite often, after school or in holiday times, the children would come down with her.

Inchmichael was coming alive with children again The numbers of my grandchildren were also increasing every year. They all called me granny irrespective of whether I was their real granny or not. The farmhouse was open house especially the kitchen. I was in my element. It was like the old days – the canary singing in its cage at the window – an art gallery of children's work and a map of the world up on the yellow kitchen walls, legions of raspberry jam on the high shelves and huge pots of soup bubbling on the Aga. There were all ages of children, babies among them. All the members of the family were married now or had partners. I still didn't agree with the partner bit but had learned to accept it.

To begin with, among the farming community, this living together unmarried, seemed to be only happening to us. It wasn't, as it transpired, but mostly other farmers' children were working or living away from home at university, whereas mine were on the doorstep. I was always quite open about it. I had learned a long time ago not to worry too much what other people said. I didn't agree with this way of living myself but I had to accept or fall out with my offspring.

Everyone was at home now working and housed on the farm

apart from Mahri who after three years in Germany with her husband was back now living in Perth. David was still with the Blackwatch but due to be demobbed soon. They had no children, so to fill the days Mahri determined to find a job. As always it was difficult for her. She had several jobs and then landed up in a Pakistani restaurant working for 'Fat Joe'. I watched her grow paler and thinner

"Mahri what hours to you work?"

"I get time off till midday but sometimes I work till two in the morning"

I whittled out more information and found out he was paying her a low wage and, what was more, wasn't paying his dues in tax and insurance for her and refused to sign a necessary form. Mahri wouldn't let me interfere until one day I said, "If you ever have to leave that job or are sacked you will be in trouble with the government. No tax has been paid."

Mahri could never bear the thought of being in any kind of trouble. "Will you go and see if you can get Joe to sign the form?" she asked. I needed no second invitation.

When I went into the restaurant he was missing as usual – a slippery customer Joe. I was confronted by a handsome Pakistani waiter carrying a tray. I told him what I required.

"Okay I'll see to it – give it to Mahri when it's signed." Put off again I thought.

"I'll come and get it tomorrow," I said, "and if I don't, there will be trouble."

I didn't get it, ofcourse. As usual when I called he wasn't available. Instead I went round to the job centre where Mahri had got the job and told my sorry tale. His business was investigated and subsequently closed down when it was discovered he was doing all sorts of illegal things. The government got the money due to them but, as is the way with these things, Mahri never got a penny.

Mahri was now at a loose end. It was high summer. Inchmichael was hotching with children. Mahri loved children, so I asked her, "How about coming down to help keep an eye on them all while their mums and dads are so busy?" She's been coming down on weekdays ever since.

Chapter 32
Cairn o' Mohr

For Ronnie and Judith, setting up a winery was more difficult than going into the shed-making business. Although more or less everything was done within the family as far as possible – plumbing, electricity, building, plastering, concrete – of necessity quite a few people from the outside world had to be involved. It had to conform to all environmental health regulations for instance. And then there was Customs and Excise. They, we thought, would be the bogey men but as it turned out, could not have been more helpful.

Somewhere to have a bond in which to keep the bottled wine had to be found. Again the old farm steading supplied the perfect place. Dark cool buildings that no one had been in for years – thick stone walls, no windows – the old meal and cake house. From one dark corner, a huge boiler had to be removed. It had once been used to boil up small potatoes – chats they were called – to mix with meal and feed to pigs. Also turnips for feeding to cattle in the winter had been stored in this place. The turnip cutter was still there and hadn't been used for years. The shed boys got busy making racks to hold wine. Henry made a strong door of steel and other things including a huge Heath Robinson sort of water boiler. It's still in use. Other necessary equipment they managed to get second hand.

"You are going to make wine," people would say. "Wine, when there are surpluses of the stuff about. Lakes of it in fact."

"Mine will be different," Ronnie would reply. "You wait and see."

There was of course a great deal of work involved. Sometimes Ronnie and Judith were at it night and day, especially in the summer months. To begin with they grew the raspberries and strawberries and collected the elderberries, oak leaves and

165

brambles from the hills and fields around. But as the winery grew bigger they gave up growing raspberries and strawberries – they just couldn't do everything. The farm boys were involved in other things and had no wish to go back into berries. Besides, there were farmers round about who could supply them with excellent fruit.

But still their forages for the fruit of the field, the woods and the hill, especially in Spring and autumn, had them coming back all tired, scratched and sunburnt.

One thing Ronnie was quite determined to grow after a while was elder trees. He began to need a lot of both berries and flowers. There were plenty wild places where the trees had a foothold but sometimes the fruit was difficult to get out. Often they had to scramble through enormous thickets of nettles or thistles – the best always seemed to grow in the most inaccessible spots. He would plant his own. He got one or two odd corners from his brothers and in every available spot in would go an elder tree – down the farm road, on the banks of the pow – everywhere.

Today we have a couple of elder tree orchards. I read somewhere they had them long long ago. Their fruits and flowers were known to be valuable for medicinal and cooking purposes but they were so common in Scotland and had the name of being a poor man's fruit, that elder went entirely out of fashion. My grandmother may have known of their usefulness but she died before I was born.

Ronald and Judith made an elderberry wine from the beginning. It was rich and dark, of an indefinable red colour. It looked wonderful before you tasted it.

One day, after being out for lunch at a neighbouring farmer's delightful restaurant, I came back raving about elderflower cordial. The whole meal had been deliciously flavoured with herbs growing in their own acres but the elderflower was the biggest surprise – cool, refreshing and a wonderful taste. I never expected it. Ronnie and Judith were looking round to make something non-alcoholic at the time. "How about elderflower cordial?" I said extolling its virtues.

They eventually developed an elderflower champagne. They

made a light brew, and had it aerated and bottled. It was bubbly and fresh like champagne. They were in business. Because of the law concerning patent, they knew they would be in trouble if they named their product champagne, but that was certainly the image it evoked. Ronnie and Judith wandered round supermarkets and wine shops looking at all the champagne bottles and chose the one they liked the best. They had a similar label made just using the word elderflower written in an attractive gold scroll and added a gold top. It looked good and tasted delicious. Later they won an award for it.

From the beginning the wine makers had an image for the wine that they intended to stick to. The first priority was it had to taste good – be good. No short cuts, no expense spared in the ingredients used. It had, of course, to obey the Customs and Excise guidelines – not over 14% alcohol or extra tax is charged. Then it had to have the right image. "We want to get away from the chateau image – this swilling in the mouth and spitting out snobbery of it all – which grape, which year, which particular wine-growing area. This is to be something different, young, fun, to be enjoyed, good for you, simply the health-giving properties of berries and what could be more natural than collecting the berries and fruit ourselves from the countryside.

"And the image we want for it also is Scottish," said Judith. Everything was discussed and thought about down to the last detail on the labels. Bottles were carefully chosen – a different one for each fruit, flower and leaf. In the beginning I helped them quite a bit. I was so enthusiastic about the wine myself that it wasn't difficult to make potential customers enthusiastic too.

Not long before they began selling it commercially I asked Ronnie what he was going to call the wine.

"We've thought long and hard about that, Mum. Castle's certainly not going to be on the label. How about Bothy?"

"Don't think so Ronnie, makes it sound too lowly." Then he came out with titles, like "Stinky stuff". It was all in vogue amongst the young at the time to disparage instead of praise.

"Don't think so," I said. "You may sell to the young but you certainly won't sell to my age group with names like that and you say you want it to appeal to all."

One day the kitchen door burst open. I was busy pouring warmed sugar into huge pots of bubbling raspberries. My annual jam making.

"What about care no more?"

"What are you talking about?"

"The name of the wine."

"Well," he spelled it out, "Cairn O' Mhor. Remember I told you there's a place in the middle of the red Australian desert called that. I named it."

"Cairn O' Mhor," I mouthed the words over to myself, thought about them.

"Have one glass and all is contentment, care has gone," said Ronnie.

"That's rather good. I kind of like that."

Ronnie, I think, was rather surprised at my approval. "Yes, I like that – it's clever, different, has a ring to it, a Scottish ring. And so Cairn O' Mohr was born.

To begin with life was fraught with difficulties. There had to be a way found of selling it to the wider public. Fortunately Michael had a friend looking for a job at the time who turned out to be an enthusiastic and excellent salesman. Cairn O' Mohr began to get known.

Things went vastly wrong sometimes. One time I remember a big batch of wine that had been bottled had started to re-ferment. I 'll never forget Judith's reaction. "It will just all have to go back into the casks."

It was ten o'clock at night when they realised the predicament but with good humour and resolve they began the huge task, working well into the night. All the time they were learning. Once a party of international experts came to give them advice and every bit of information was noted. But again experience was the best teacher. A lesson once learned through experience was never forgotten.

Chapter 33

Lindsay

People still say to me from time to time when they learn of the size of my family, "Seven children – how on earth did you manage?" I reply, "It's not difficult really. They're not all babies or infants at the same time and the first half of the family help to bring up the second half."

Time whizzes by too. It seemed no time at all from when I was pushing my most welcome and wanted sixth baby in the new pedigree pram up the hill to Errol to when he was a tall slim youth of seventeen with reddish brown hair and the blue eyes of his father. He had also his rather nervous disposition along with the same determination to take no notice of an inherent condition but just barge on regardless.

Like his older brother Ronnie a lot of Lindsay's teenage leisure time was spent up in the village with his friends. From time to time he got into a bit of bother along with the other boys. Daring ideas were hatched out on the school bus but they were all country boys and there was no serious trouble.

Lindsay had actually stayed on a little longer at school than the rest of them and got qualifications that would have taken him to university. But like the others, he wanted to get on with life – have the adventures his brothers were having.

It wasn't long till he was up in Richard's flat in Aberdeen and had got an oil-related job. He got good pay for a young lad. I felt it was too good, it would give him wrong ideas of how hard it could be to make a living – a false sense of security. It did however, give him the where-with-all to travel and that's what he wanted to do – see the world as his brothers had done before him.

He took full advantage of the years of cheap travel as so many other young people were doing at the time and, of course being young, spurned the idea of package holidays. They were for tourists – the elderly. The young didn't see themselves as tourists. They were explorers of a world opening out for them.

How different it was for my generation. It was difficult for us to travel abroad, especially if we were teenagers in the aftermath of the second world war. For me, on two pounds a week, the meagre wages of a nurse, it was impossible to save enough to go anywhere apart from bicycling holidays around Scotland sleeping in youth hostels. Ronald and I liked the idea of young folk exploring and encouraged it when we could.

They always knew that they could come back here if things went wrong and get in touch at any time. That none of them ever did get in touch when they were in trouble astounds me to this day. Quite often they did run into real difficulties but always managed to arrive home with rucksacks of dirty washing (which they didn't expect me to launder. They had long been taught otherwise) and rolls of toilet paper. We didn't always like their mode of transport but usually didn't know about it till afterwards. It was always the cheapest. The Magic Bus from London to Greece for twenty five pounds was an example. I wasn't told much about it before Lindsay left but afterwards, when I was told, I thought the only thing magic about it was that it ever reached its destination at all. But arrive it did.

"The whole journey is quite an adventure," Lindsay told me after coming home from one of these trips.

"See when we crossed the border into Yugoslavia. The Brits among us didn't know what was happening. Half the Yugoslavs got off the bus and handed us bags stuffed with jeans. Then the guards got on. Every one was searched but we were okay. We were allowed to carry more or less, what we wanted to. The Yugoslavs were not allowed to bring jeans into the country. After the search the guards got off. A bit further down the road the young Yugoslavs got on again and reclaimed their plastic bags."

The boys were certainly learning about life and I along with them. I had always wanted to travel 'just to see' as an Irish lady traveller had once said to me. Apart from our Canada adventure and once or twice to Tenerife when the farm was doing a little better than usual, I had not been out of the country. But now I was travelling vicariously through the family. I was always eager to hear of their adventures and the independent way that they travelled gave them many.

When they got to the country of their choice they looked for work – anything that would give them enough money to let them stay and explore before moving on. Like his brothers before him, Lindsay visited many places – Spain, Israel, Greece – and got seasonal work. There were certain little restaurants and cafés where farmers came to look for foreign labour when they needed pickers for tomatoes, apricots, oranges or olives. The young travellers learned of these places from each other. They also gleaned a lot of information relevant to them from *The Lonely Planet Guide* a battered copy of which could be found in most rucksacks. It was a very different sort of life from package holidays but they were prepared to rough it – sleep anywhere – out in the olive groves or on beaches swept by warm seas.

"Did I tell you about the time I was selling melons on the beach in Greece? I hadn't had a good day. I was short of money. I went to sleep on the beach. I was really tired and slept like a log. When I woke up in the morning my melons and the little money that I had were gone. Oh my melons – oh my money!"

"And what did you do?" I asked, my voice edged with anxiety.

"Oh I had friends. They helped me out till I got a better job picking apricots. We all help each other out. There's a tremendous camaraderie amongst us all – it's great."

At one point later on, Lindsay followed Grant to Canada's North West Territories. Like the rest of them he had heard Ronald and I talk of our adventures in Canada before he was born – and had been inspired to see it for himself. He lived there for one bright summer but wasn't sure if he could handle the severe winter and possible lack of company.

"What did you think when you first arrived there?" I asked him one day.

"It was early in May. Grant met me in Edmonton where he had been taking a short holiday. We started on the long journey north. It would take us three days at least. It was close on a thousand miles to Lindberg's Landing. The distances amazed me. We seemed to be travelling for ever but there was much of interest to see in northern Alberta. After we eventually reached a small place called Enterprise near to where the road branches off to Hay River, there was nothing but trees and more trees – fir trees mostly which you couldn't see over or through. However the skies were brilliantly blue and the sun shone all day. I couldn't get over the clarity of the air. I had not a care in the world. I thought it would be all plain sailing. I had come thousands of miles – only three hundred or so more to go. Grant had said the Mackenzie highway was a good road. I've never in my life been on a lonelier one. It seemed to be never coming to an end – no houses, no gas station, just trees and more trees. Half way along Grant's truck broke down. We both know a bit about motors but very soon realised it was unfixable without a certain tool we hadn't got.

" 'What do we do now, Grant?' I said.

" 'We'll just have to wait till someone comes along.'

" 'When will that be?' I asked. 'We haven't seen one vehicle of any kind since the turn-off to Yellowknife.'

" 'Normally,' said Grant, 'there are several trucks on the road heading for the ferry that goes to Fort Simpson. Perhaps I've misjudged things a bit. The ice roads that we use all winter have broken up but maybe the reason there's no traffic is that the ferry can't operate yet as there are still chunks of ice floating down the river. Don't worry though, something will turn up.'

"Grant didn't seem at all concerned but I couldn't help thinking of the black bears I had seen at the side of the road and how cold it was at night even if it was May. Besides I was hungry. But Grant's optimism paid off. Within an hour a truck approached us and stopped.

" 'You guy's having problems?'

" 'Sure are,' replied Grant and told him what ailed the truck.

" 'Perhaps I can fix it. Can fix most things these days. Have tools in my truck. Fact, I'm on the way up north to fix the Fort Simpson Ferry. It'll soon be sailing time again. Any day now the river will be flowing free of ice.'

"But even after poking about in the innards of Grant's truck for quite some time and the use of some choice, picturesque, blasphemic language that made me smile in spite of the predicament we were in, he said, 'No, I can't fix the goddamn thing. It's got me beat. Tell you what, I'll give you a lift to the ferry. Where you guys heading for anyway?'

" 'Lindberg's Landing,' said Grant.

" 'It's getting nearer," said the truck driver. 'Jump in.'

"He let us off on the road still about eighty miles short of Lindberg's Landing.

" 'What do we do now?' I asked.

" 'Dunno,' said Grant. 'You know how he is, Mum, a lad of few words. 'Not much chance of any trucks passing now, but don't worry something'll turn up.'

"Shortly after he said that we heard a loud droning above.

" 'Quick!' said Grant, sparked into instant action for once, 'Get off the road.'

"I hadn't time to look up. I scarpered into the trees. Down came a small plane, a Cessna on to the road just where we had been standing a moment before. I hadn't particularly noticed but we had been standing on a part of the straight-snake-road where it bulges out for a space. These bulges recur at intervals on the Mackenzie highway for use as emergency air strips for planes to use should they get into trouble. There is nowhere else to land. They can't land on trees or muskeg. The bush pilot who stepped out of the cockpit seemed equally surprised to see us.

" 'What you guys doing here?'

"We explained our plight.

" 'Take you over the river to Fort Simpson if that's any help,' he offered. 'Once I get this goddamn plane fixed. I'm on the grocery run there while the river's unstable.'

"We remained in Fort Simpson for a day or two until the river was clear and the ferry was running again. Ed Lindberg came to collect us. It was late but still light when we arrived at Lindberg's Landing. The following day we were up early. Ed had work he wanted us to do. I was out on the sunlit porch waiting for him enjoying just looking and listening. The birds were singing – the trees coming into their spring greenery – everything so fresh and clean and silent – the air so clear. Suddenly the screen door, that keeps the flies and mosquitoes at bay, swung open and out barged Ed. Without saying anything and made for the hen run at the side of the house not far from the swollen Liard river. He was carrying a gun. I hadn't noticed before but just beside the hen run, half hidden by trees, I saw a black bear.

"Ed lifted the gun to shoulder level – the gun went off – in the clear air the din was deafening and the next thing I knew the bear lay still on the ground.

" 'Got the bastard at last,' said Ed. 'It's sure been mooling about the hens recently, a danger to all of us when it starts hanging around like that. Here,' he said, throwing me a rope he'd picked of the ground, 'tie this round the bastard's neck and I'll get the tractor and haul it away.'

" 'Who me?' I said stunned by his demand

" 'Yes, you.' I didn't want to disobey his first order – what would he think of me? But how could I be sure the bear was dead – perhaps it was only stunned and would get up and grab me the moment I got to it. In fear and trepidation I approached. I can tell you I booted its arse a few times to make sure it was dead before I went near its head. I gingerly put the noose round its neck. It didn't move. But my first job in Canada left me shaking from head to foot. In spite of the shock, I couldn't help thinking what a beautiful creature it was.

"Just the same it wasn't that sort of thing that brought me back and there's plenty of work there. It was just everything – in the summer mosquitoes and other flies, big ones they call bulldogs and little ones they call no-see-ums, that bite the hell out of you – the long freezing winter, but mostly I think the lack of company of my own age – people who are on the same wavelength as myself. Grant can handle it, seems to like it but I don't think I could."

Lindsay went back to the oilrigs for the winter but by Spring he was not well again. The resin that he worked with, although he wore the regulation masks, went for his lungs – he had difficulty in breathing. He came home for a while to recuperate.

"How about a job on the farm?" I said, There's plenty of work at the moment and perhaps we could start up some other aspect of farming that would give you a more permanent job?"

Lindsay agreed and he did try. It was the time of year for

cultivating the land. It meant long strenuous and monotonous hours on a tractor, up and down, up and down the long drills, always watching, always concentrating carefully in order to do the job properly. Lindsay was a perfectionist.

"Can't handle it," said Lindsay one day. "But I'm feeling fit again. Some of my pals are off to Australia. I'll see if I can get a work permit for a year like Ronnie did – he liked it well enough – see what happens – might stay there," and he was gone.

Like Ronnie before him he had many adventures in Australia. Ironically his first job was on a wheat farm in an even more remote place than Lindberg's

"Ed lifted the gun to shoulder level – the gun went off – in the clear air the din was deafening and the next thing I knew the bear lay still on the ground."

Landing in South Western Australia. However this job was short-lived. On the very first day Lindsay inadvertently broke the farmer's combine harvester and the farmer flew into a terrible rage. It would need a new part costing two thousand dollars which would have to come from a town four hundred miles away. Lindsay fled from the farmer's wrath. He had been told that one bus passed on the highway on a Saturday, that was all. This was only Monday. Just the same Lindsay thought he would take a chance. He waited by the side of the dusty road that melted into a heat haze many miles further on. He stood a full day in 40^0 of heat before finally the third car he'd seen gave him a lift taking him the five hundred miles back to Perth.

After that episode he did many jobs across Australia and ended up painting a stadium roof in Sydney. However he came up with no job that would have allowed him to stay longer in Australia once his work permit ran out.

"What are you planning to do now?" I asked when he returned home.

"Perhaps I'll see If I can get into Dundee University" I've got the required qualifications. A friend of mine is a teacher and he quite likes it." And so in the autumn Lindsay went to Dundee

University. He enjoyed the work especially the English. I was surprised how good he was at it. I hadn't realised what talent lay hidden there, but after six months he gave it all up.

"Can't handle it," he said to me one day. "I just can't handle sitting all day at books. I feel I just must have physical work to keep my nerves from jumping. Maybe I've been away too long from studying."

That spring Grant and the shed boys were very busy. Desperate for help they asked Lindsay if he would work for them for a while.

"Sure I'll give it a go." Lindsay was a fast learner and loved the work

"Why not join us permanently?" Grant asked Lindsay one day.

"Okay then," said Lindsay, "I will." He's been there ever since.

Chapter 34
Kathleen

If Lindsay seemed to grow up quickly, my youngest child, Kathleen appeared to grow up even quicker. Like Topsy, she just grew. We became, from an early age, good friends. She was outgoing and easy to get on with, at least within the family. When younger, with girls of her own age, she would say one week, "She's my best friend – always will be." And the next week, "I hate her, I hate her. I'm never going to speak to her again as long as I live." But you knew they would be best friends again soon.

She occasionally got angry about things and we would all say, "Calm down, Kathleen. Your red hair is getting in your eyes." She was the only member of the family to have auburn hair and blue eyes. When young she played mostly with her older brothers and, as far as they were concerned, had one great asset that girls didn't usually have – she never told on them whatever they were doing. Therefore she was allowed in their gang huts hidden in the back yard or the orchard. She didn't play at 'house' much. I had hoped to keep Kathleen in about a bit longer but no way.

A month or two before she was seventeen she was off to Aberdeen to seek her fortune. Lindsay was still living there along with a few of their friends. Richard had not as yet sold his flat and that was where all the fun was. Kathleen loved fun and parties and the company of people her own age. I wasn't too worried as her ideas were sensible but I worried about the times she was living in.

Kathleen was a very different girl to her sister Mahri. Mahri was quite content to conform to the ways in which I was brought up. Mahri wanted to be protected by the family. Kathleen did not.

"Mum, don't you dare come and collect me from the disco.

I'll just die of embarrassment if you do! I'll get a taxi – don't worry. I'm perfectly capable of looking after myself." Kathleen was an independent girl – truly of the new generation. Before she left for Aberdeen I tried to instil into her some of my values but knowing all the time that she would have to go, to a certain extent, her own way. I was well aware that revolution by the young was nothing new. It had been going on since time began.

I had revolted against some of my mother's ideas. My mother hadn't wanted me to go in for nursing which she considered too menial a task for her daughter. I argued endlessly over racism or any divisions in society – everyone was equal and in some areas things *had* improved. I had welcomed my mother's modern ideas – "There is nothing a women can't do – there is no such word as can't in the dictionary," she had always said.

How many artists, writers, composers or scientists had been lost to the world because of taboos on women doing anything outside the home? However, with the advent and easy availability of the contraceptive pill it seemed to me that, what had been a gradual liberation of women had taken a step too far. The more and more common occurrence of young men and women living together unmarried came late to the farms and villages and was difficult for the older generation to accept.

It seemed to be an erosion of all the principles we held most dear. Now with the pill, no longer need the woman be left holding the baby. She was truly liberated. "Like men" it was said, but what was freedom? Were men free? "Shades of the prison house surround the growing boy." The words of Wordsworth ran through my head. In my view the family was the most important institution – the building block of society. Now the family was becoming secondary. "What work do you do?" was asked of women. Look after the family, for women of independent mind, was not the correct answer.

Kathleen did find it difficult in Aberdeen – very difficult to find work without specific qualifications but eventually she found a job in community education, getting young girls off the streets and into clubs.

Once Henry and I went up to Aberdeen to take her out for a meal. To our older eyes, her appearance was slightly shocking.

She was wearing all the modern gear with her hair wild and uncombed as was the fashion at the time.

"Why don't girls make the best of their looks not the worst of them?" I wondered to myself but didn't say. When questioned about her appearance she said, "I dress how all young people dress today. It reflects a non-conformist attitude. Young people are rebelling against being 'sensible'. Besides if I dressed differently I would have no rapport with the young people I work with. They wouldn't trust me."

After getting a paid occupation Kathleen's next ambition was to travel.

"I've got a return ticket to Turkey," she told me one day when she paid one of her brief visits home. Elspeth and I are off next month." Elspeth was a new friend whom I hadn't met.

"Oh Katy! Why Turkey and where will you be staying?"

"Dunno," she said. "We'll find somewhere. We're flying to Daliman. I mentioned package deals but this was anathema to the young – only for the old, I was told, and that meant anyone over twenty five according to Kathleen. I wasn't, however, too worried about her travelling ability.

Once, when she came with me to see Mahri in Germany, we had nearly been in real difficulty over tickets for the train to take us to the airport. We ran out of foreign currency and nearly missed our flight. I was much more worried than Kathleen was.

"I'll sort it out, Mum," she said and did.

As promised I got a postcard from Turkey – "Having a wonderful time – white mountains – brilliantly blue lakes – very eastern and different – you'd love it."

When she came back I asked a lot of questions. They'd found the people very hospitable and easily found a place to stay.

"But the men, Kathleen?" I asked, having heard of these eastern, warm-blooded types and their relationships with western women who, in their estimation, had fallen low.

"If ever we felt threatened, I developed a nervous twitch in my neck and Elspeth started talking to someone in the sky. They soon thought we were clearly mad and avoided us like the plague."

Kathleen's next adventure with her friend Elspeth was to

India. This time for a longer stay. She kind of knew what to expect, having listened to her brother Ronnie's experiences, but she was horrified, just the same, at how the poor had to live. She learned of things that were almost inconceivable to her having been brought up in a secure home. How it had been the custom, and still was practised to an extent, for widows to be thrown out of their homes often with their children. Sometimes life was so desperate for them that they sold their children cheaply to people who maimed them and used them as beggars. Kathleen told me how different life was for the youngsters she was in charge of.

"Last time I took them to the pictures they moaned and groaned because I was delayed by traffic and was five minutes late."

"You should have told them that in India they would have been sold for less than the price of mutton."

"Aw, Mum," she said in her 'you just don't understand' kind of voice.

Sometime later Kathleen changed her job. She took up work in one of Aberdeen's night shelters. I was pleased that she was doing such necessary work but apprehensive also.

"Who comes into these places? What sort of people?"

"People who are down on their luck and without homes. Sometimes drug addicts, or alcoholics, unlucky people."

"Are some of them not dangerous?"

"Not really," said Kathleen. "The shelter is their last place of refuge. They're unlikely to attack us." She did admit however that her job could be stressful at times. It helped, that at a dance hall, she met a boy, red-haired like herself and about her own age. They got on well together and fell in love. His name was Rab. Rab was a great climber in the Scottish mountains. There was nothing he enjoyed more.

"What are you going to do for a living?" Kathleen had asked him one day.

"Oh something will turn up," he said and it did. Some of his friend had formed a company to work on the oil rigs. They were abseilers – they could abseil up and down anything, a very useful skill to have as far as the oil companies were concerned. They were employed more and more to paint, do minor repairs, or weld in inaccessible places. Rab went to work with them.

After a while Rab and Kathleen decided to take advantage of a cheap round the world trip for the exploring young. The plan was to spend a year away and explore the places they arrived in. India was their first destination. Kathleen wanted to show Rab the country she had fallen in love with – "nowhere more alive," she told him. On arrival they headed for Nepal, travelling by bus. Buses in India were always filled to capacity. "If you can hang on you can get on" was the ruling. Inside the bus, with so many other people they felt like sardines in a tin and it was stifling. At every stop they noticed someone get out to climb on the roof. Soon they did likewise and found it a much better way to travel. The roofrack was palatial compared to inside the bus, rucksacks and bags made good mattresses and pillows.

"The greatest bus journey of my life," Kathleen told me after she got home. "The views were breathtaking – the snow-capped mountains of the Himalayas cutting into the deep blue sky. Even more breathtaking, the sheer cliff drops on the sharp corners seen from the roofrack. Later they were told they were in the best place if the bus tipped over a precipice – and it did happen from time to time – you could always jump off!

Rab and Kathleen stayed in Nepal for a month exploring the mountain paths and hill towns along the way. That is where Kathleen thought she caught the illness that was to plague her off and on for some time to come.

After Nepal they journeyed south to Varanasi in India. It was election time there and fighting had flared up between Hindus and Muslims. Wanting to protect the tourists the Indians shepherded them to safe accommodation as soon as they alighted from the bus. Fortunately the troubles were nearly over by the time they got to Varanasi.

"Oddly, Mum," Kathleen told me at a later date, "Amidst all the chaos I found more peace there than anywhere else in India. The holy Ganges runs close to Varanasi. As you know I'm not of a religious nature but the Ganges held a spirit of some kind. There was a feeling of peace there as soon as you approached the river. When we sat on its banks a low fog hovered over the river muffling sound. Men in long boats appeared and slowly disappeared into the distance. Two fresh water porpoises skimmed the surface of the water bringing life into a river used for death. At the side of the river women washed their clothes beside fires where loved ones were cremated. It sounds crazy but somehow it's not."

At Varanasi Kathleen became ill but didn't like the sound of the doctors she heard about so Rab and she travelled by train to the bigger city of Delhi. Kathleen was so ill and weak with diarrhoea by the end of the journey that Rab had to carry her to the toilet and back. The doctor in Delhi diagnosed dysentery and prescribed antibiotics.

Kathleen recovered quickly and Rab and she took a trip riding on camels through what seemed like an endless and barren desert to a sandstone castle and a town where stalls were laid out with brightly coloured turbans and lengths of cloth reflecting the rich colours of the landscape. Kathleen began to feel ill again. They returned to Delhi by camel and decided to leave India because of Kathleen's health problems. They flew to Thailand and a doctor in Bangkok diagnosed Jardia – "a disease," he told them, "that is hard to detect because of the way it comes and goes." Again she was put on medication and recovered although by this time she was scarecrow thin.

She kept reasonably well for a while and after exploring Thailand they travelled on to Malaysia. In Singapore Kathleen took ill again and landed in a hospital bed. "Perhaps you have bowel cancer," the doctors suggested. "We'll have to operate to find out." Rab refused to allow this. Again, medication and she began to recover.

It was in this hospital bed in Singapore that Rab proposed to Kathleen. "Lets get out of here first" was Kathleen's reply.

They travelled to Australia and saw a doctor there. They told him what the Singapore opinion had been.

"The only thing these doctors thought you had was a good health insurance policy," he replied. Gradually Kathleen began to feel stronger and the bouts of Jardia waned. But her troubles weren't over yet.

On a far flung beach bordering the coral reefs she stepped

on the tail spike of a dangerous stingray. Quickly her whole leg blew up to an enormous size. The doctor shook his head – "Not Good" and stuck in an enormous needle. Gradually the swelling went down. At this point they nearly came home.

We got a phone call from Australia telling us nothing of their troubles only – rejoice, rejoice, rejoice – they had become engaged. Things improved after that. They got work in Australia for a while – Kathleen endlessly licking stamps, before flying to New Zealand. Postcards arrived from that country saying they were on a tour with other young people and what fun it was – what a beautiful country and how well they were treated by everyone.

A year later they were married and managed to buy an attractive old house – a keeper's lodge, near a lonely village in Aberdeenshire where they lived for several years. But after the arrival of their daughter, Jasmin, things became too difficult with the remoteness of the place, the likelihood of heavy snowstorms in winter and Rab being away so often on the rigs. Due to the nature of Rab's work it didn't really matter where he lived.

"How about moving to the Carse of Gowrie?" Kathleen suggested.

After selling up they lived with us in the farm house for six months while looking for a house in the Carse. The houses they looked at were all very expensive and nothing suitable turned up. Eventually they applied and got permission to build a house at East Inchmichael. Now, apart from Mahri, who lived in Perth but came down on weekdays to be with us, every one was home again.

Chapter 35

Microlite

There were many qualities in Henry that I liked and admired. His total honesty was one of them and he lacked any sort of pretension. Like me he had never any wish to keep up with the Joneses. If he wanted something it was for its own sake.

He also had a sense of adventure which he had never lost. If there was a boring road to take or an exciting one he would always take the exciting one which matched my wishes too. When we were married Henry had one great passion that I wasn't altogether aware of. He liked flying and particularly in a microlite. For the past few years he had been flying in one belonging to a friend. He had done quite a bit of flying himself. According to Henry it was the most wonderful sport in the world, a sport for kings.

"Isn't it dangerous?" I asked.

"Not at all," he would say. "Not if you watch what you are doing and choose the right weather to go up in."

According to Henry every other kind of flying was more dangerous. I wasn't altogether convinced but when the chance to buy a second hand microlite came up, I encouraged him to get it, despite my foreboding. At the time there was very little else he wanted out of life. I just loved to see him happy.

"Until I'm really expert at it," he said, "I'll only fly over the farm." I worried about the jets that sometimes came screaming over but Henry assured me he wouldn't be high enough to get in their way.

I had never seen a microlite before nor had anyone in the district. On his first flight I couldn't help thinking what a strange and beautiful thing. With its wide triangular wings it looked more like some great prehistoric bird than a modern-day aeroplane. Henry dangled beneath it like some prey caught in its claws. It was much watched for and remarked upon by everyone around. To begin with I enjoyed watching him and then one day in late summer, a day of blue skies over the Carse but with a bit of an autumnal breeze, Henry took off from the twice shorn hay field that he called the airfield. A fresh gust of wind caught the microlite before it had gained its usual height. Suddenly it took on a life of its own, twisted round and plummeted back to earth and looked as though it was ploughing up the burned down shaws of the tattie field before it came to a halt. Brother-in-law John was with

> "Today
> the air
> is like silk.
> I think
> I'll have
> a flight."

me at the time. It was so like something out of a Laurel and Hardy film that he couldn't help laughing. He had an infectious laugh and I couldn't help laughing either, although running towards Henry I had fear in my heart.

He was perfectly all right. Much more concerned about the broken bits in the microlite than anything that might have happened to himself. After that I was even more anxious and decided not to watch. When I knew he was flying, I put one of the family on alert. The boys liked to watch.

"You should really come and look now," Lindsay said to me one day. "Henry's getting really good at it." But I preferred not to.

One bright summer morning early Henry said to me, "Today the air is like silk. I think I'll have a flight." Lindsay was around at the time just about to do some disliked cultivating of the grain.

"Okay," I said, "I'll get on with my typing for a while." It didn't seem ten minutes since he had gone when I heard a commotion in the kitchen. I hurried through to find Judith, Lindsay and Henry. I took one look at Henry. His left arm was at a most peculiar angle and bleeding. "I was coming round the corner in the truck when I saw it come down," said Judith. "We'll need to take him straight to hospital because of the bleeding. I've put on a tourniquet so Lindsay can drive. I'll go with him."

Henry refused to go in anything but the truck. "I'll make far too much mess of the car," he said. Although you could see he was in considerable pain he was remarkably calm about it all and in no time he was off in the two seater truck. Judith jumped into the back. "DRI," she shouted. "You can follow in the car." Before I left the farm road they were out of sight flying towards Dundee. I went flying off in the opposite direction. I thought she had shouted PRI – Perth Royal Infirmary – the hospital we usually went to.

When I got there and rushed into casualty I could hardly believe they hadn't arrived.

"But they must have done," I said. "I saw them go, I didn't pass them on the road, it's my husband – he's badly injured."

"Not here," said the girl at reception. "We haven't had any casualties through these doors since six o'clock this morning. Are you sure it isn't the DRI." Slowly it began to dawn – the possibility.

"I'll give them a phone," the nurse said. "Yes they've just had someone in with a badly injured arm. Said he fell off a ladder or something."

"Fell off a ladder." Still I wasn't totally convinced but got in the car and hot pedalled it for Dundee. I didn't see him to begin with. He had been taken immediately into theatre. They were operating on him right away.

"He might have a badly damaged arm but he'll be okay," Judith assured me.

"What happened?" I asked.

An unexpected wind got up not long after take off. He hadn't enough height when it happened. The microlite got out of control, came back to earth and as misfortune would have it, it hit about the only post left on Inchmichael.

Later I heard the rest. How Lindsay had flown into Dundee at about 100 miles an hour with Judith in the back, hair streaming in the wind.

"Don't tell them about the microlite," she said, "if you don't want to risk headlines in the paper. Who knows? It might be a slow news day. Say you fell off a ladder."

The doctors looked a bit sceptical at the explanation of such massive arm injuries but like all good doctors didn't question further and accepted the explanation.

"Some fall," they said.

They took the greatest care of him. He was in the hospital for three weeks but when he came out things looked a lot healthier, although his arm took a long time to heal properly.

One mystery remained.

"Whatever happened to my watch?" asked Henry.

One day we went down to have a look at the dreaded culprit of a post. There was the watch embedded in the wood.

The microlite was also pretty much broken up but Henry laboriously sorted it. I was fearful about him going up again but eventually he sold it. I think partly because he knew it worried me so much. He still maintains they are not really dangerous.

And some bright mornings when we are out together walking round the fields he will say, "The air is like silk today," and I know just what he is thinking.

Chapter 36

Peace to Write

Over the years the chapel at Inchmichael, from time to time, was a great place to escape to. An actress, I can't remember who, who had a big family, was once asked how she managed to cope. "I have a big house and I hide a lot," was her answer. I lived in much the same way. If I wanted to get a bit of writing done, I had one or two bolt holes.

One was the chapel. It was always so peaceful. Another was the attic with its sloping roof. I made it into a makeshift office. It had a skylight and a small window on the gable end of the house looking towards the hills. From time to time apples were stored here so it had the faint smell of apples and the distant sounds of life going on downstairs, low enough not to be disturbing. My favourite place for writing however, was the kitchen, either early in the morning at five or six before anyone was up, or in the middle of the night when I would wake up with an idea and need to get it down before I forgot. It was always warm in the kitchen with the Aga on nine months of the year. The attic and chapel were good in the summer. In the attic I loved to hear the rain on the roof or when there was a high wind, pretend I was in a ship at sea and miles from anywhere.

However I did feel the chapel was such a special place. I would like to use it more. There were no laws against you using it privately and so began my Annual Writers Party early in May. It began quite modestly with just the Perthshire group members attending and then I thought why not mix everyone together and so the members of the groups I attended in Dundee were invited too. In fact it became a sort of open house for any writer who wanted to come.

The numbers at the party grew. It was a lovely time of year to come out into the country with everything so green. Any guest who wanted brought a short piece to read out – a poem, short story or article. We provided stovies and wine. It wasn't too expensive. I had huge pots in which to make the stovies and Cairn O' Mohr bought from the winery at family prices. Everyone said how much they enjoyed these nights.

Over these years I had two more collections of poetry published, one by Brenda Shaw with her Blind Serpent Press and the other with Duncan Glen. Then at last the book about our adventures in Canada got published. Glory, glory, glory. The harder it is to get something you really want, the more rejoicing there is when it happens. I could hardly believe it. I'd left my new version incomplete for a long time. Then one day Jean Ramsay, a writing friend, asked how my revised version of the Canada book was progressing.

"Not very well," I said, "There always seems to be so many other things to do."

"It's not that at all," she said, "it's too much gallivanting that's the trouble." That was certainly part of it. Since Henry and I got married we were travelling quite a bit. I told Henry what Jean said.

"I'll tell you what," he said, "how about taking a winter holiday this year – going away for January, February to Majorca, say. You could finish writing your book there away from all disturbances." We looked around at the various travel agents and came up with a good deal. Eight weeks at an unknown hotel in Santo Ponza for £200 each, flight and all. We booked. Henry, as always, was trying to help me in every way he could. He had hit it off this time. We landed at the Holiday Centre – not a very prepossessing name, I thought, but it turned out a perfect place to write a book. Later I called it the rabbit warren. It had little balconies all over the place and no one looked directly into another. In the winter months it was mostly pensioners who inhabited the apart-ments.They sat out on their sunny balconies, or lower down at their front doors, all day long just enjoying the sun. I was on my sunny balcony in the morning, busily writing. In the afternoons Henry and I went walking along the many wonderful country roads with the almond blossom in full flower, the orange and lemon groves bright with ripe fruit hanging from the trees.

When I got back home to Scotland I put what I had written up on the Amstrad, printed a typescript and sent it out hopefully again. I sent the full ms this time to two publishers. Back they both came – had they even looked at them? The letters of rejection seemed even more impersonal – with "nothing autobiographical unless you are very very famous" – two "verys" I noticed now. I was really disheartened this time and did nothing more for a while. Then one day an unexpected circumstance took over.

By this time I was a member of PEN (Poets, Essayists and Novelists). They had produced a book *A Scottish Feast,* an anthology of works around the subjects of food and eating. I had a poem included. Invitations were sent to the book launches in both Edinburgh and Glasgow. I decided to go to the Edinburgh one. Henry came with me. Argyll publishing had produced the book and its editor Derek Rodger was there. Henry had a conversation with him and liked him. At the meeting too I met Simon Berry the acting president of PEN. He asked, as a favour, if seeing as it was for a good cause, would we come through to the Glasgow meeting and bring with us the case of Cairn O' Mohr wine he had ordered from Ronnie for the occasion. A bit unwillingly I agreed as we would be busy on the farm at that time. After the Edinburgh meeting when Henry was telling me about his conversation with Derek Rodger I said, "I should have told him about my book – asked him if he would consider publication."

"You should," said Henry.

We took the wine to Glasgow. Derek was there again.

"Do you think I should ask him," I said to Henry.

"Yes go on. He can only say no."

I got a chance to speak to him plucked up courage. I told him about the book. Much to my astonishment he said he might be interessted. "Send me the MS. I'll read it let you know."

I heard nothing for three months. I had, I admit, completely given up hope when a letter arrived.

A belated thank you for sending me the above on July 4.
This looks like an amazing story of youth and energy,

190

hope and love. You must have been in love just to
survive it! I am sorry it has taken three months to get to
it. It is very well written but at 100,000 words I can see
that it might benefit from being condensed in places.
It could be a commercial proposition.

Later, over the phone, he told me he intended bringing it out in
hardback. I could hardly believe it!

Chapter 37
Travel

With the farm and businesses up and running I was less needed at home. And with the money Henry made from his manufacturing line in wood stoves and the interest I saved from money my father and an aunt had left me, for the first time in our lives we had the time and the wherewithal to travel. Both being of a thrifty nature we always looked for the cheapest deals – the best value for money.

Why this compulsion to travel? Perhaps it differs for everyone and at different stages in life the need changes for individuals too. For Henry and I, no longer was it fuelled by the yearning of youth that things just might be better somewhere else – that there were better lands than this where life would be easier, where any skills we had would be more appreciated. I, for one, was glad that I had not remained in Canada in the early years. Much more than three years there and I might have developed too great an affection for the country and never been quite sure where I really wanted to be. Had I remained in Canada I think I would always have had a sad sense of alienation at being exiled from the country of my roots and youthful memories

> Oh! Rowan tree, Oh! Rowan tree
> Thoul't aye be dear tae me
> Intwin'd thou art
> Wi mony ties o hame and infancy.

For centuries Scots have travelled. Often, in the past, to escape from poverty. Opportunities looked brighter in some distant land we had heard of. Certainly, sometimes they were and many transplanted Scots did well elsewhere.

Perhaps when it comes down to holiday travel, the desire to

get away to the sun is one of the strongest motives. There are years when we see so little of it in this northern land. Oh the joy of being in the sun, even if it is not always a warm one. Nothing lifts the spirit like this.

But it was neither the wish to find a better land nor the search for the sun that was the main reason for wanting to travel now. I simply wanted to see for myself what other places were like. Just as when young, I wanted to read books, I wanted to know how other people lived, wanted to have vicarious adventure, the world described to me. Now I wanted it for real. Perhaps I didn't realise this was my main reason for wanting to travel until one day I met in Majorca a small Irish lady, insignificantly dressed – a pensioner of indomitable spirit.

"It was neither the wish to find a better land nor the search for the sun that was the main reason for wanting to travel now. I simply wanted to see for myself."

"I just want to see," the Irish lady told me. "I'm a pensioner. I live in a retirement complex. I have very little money but I save up every penny. I know I must eat to keep healthy but otherwise I spend very little and always find the cheapest deals. Every year I go somewhere different."

She was most upset one day when I met her.

"I've been on the same trip twice," she said, "the second time they called it by a different name. I didn't know."

I wasn't quite so obsessive about always having to see somewhere new. If I really liked a place I was content to return but at last after meeting the Irish lady I had defined my main reason for wanting to travel.

There were other times, of course, when things had been so hectic at home that I wanted away for a little peace – a bit of space for Henry and I and again it was while in Majorca that this was well explained to me in a passage from *Winter in Majorca* by George Sands. She was a French writer but, living in the nineteenth century, had thought it more expedient to assume a man's name. She had indeed spent one memorable winter in Majorca with the ailing Chopin in the middle of the last century. The words of the passage I read stayed with me.

> In my case I set off to satisfy a need for rest, which I particularly felt at the time. Because there is not time for everything in the world that we have made, I imagined yet again, that if I looked carefully, I would find some quiet, isolated retreat where I would have no notes to write, no newspapers to read or visitors to receive, where I would never have to take off my dressing gown, where every day would last twelve hours and where I could free myself from the duties of polite society. Which of us has not selfishly dreamed of leaving, one fine morning, all his affairs, his habits, his acquaintances and even his friends, to go to some enchanted island and live without cares, without troubles, without obligations, and above all without newspapers?

For me, another reason for travelling was to get fresh inspiration to write poetry because that was my chief love. I would get fascinated by something, say the story of George Sands, take notes, write while I was there, but also, after I got home I would go to a library, and get more information. I wrote a sequence of poems on George Sands and Chopin and, after a holiday in Cyprus, one on Makarious. The places gave me insight into people's characters I would otherwise not have had.

I often wrote poems on the spot – immediate impressions. I loved to describe place and colour – the essence of everything. I could not have written about these places cold. I had to feel this essence. I also liked to write about people whom we met by chance from many different lands and from all walks of life. I liked to write about the adventurous things that happened along the way and the amusing things. For me to write down what most interested me, for some reason, gave me great pleasure.

I also toyed with the idea of writing novels when I got back home – often romantic novels. I got a wealth of ideas. For instance that pretty courier girl in Turkey with the Scottish accent who had fallen for a handsome Turk – a student doctor turned courier for the summer in order to pay for his training. We heard how he had taken her, with great difficulty, over swamp and rivers in spate, up the side of a steep mountain to see the eternal flame coming from the peak of Olympus.

"The real Olympus," he told her. "Its flame never goes out." But it had. It had been so very wet the rain had doused it. The girl wanted him to go back for a match to re-light it – what a basis for a story that would have made. But not one I wrote. Returning home there was never enough peace or time.

To begin with it was mainly warm islands that we made for. We chose off-peak times to go. Retired and semi-retired people have this advantage. However we also visited larger land masses from time to time. From Cyprus we took a most memorable three day trip to Israel and Egypt on the *Romantica* that years later came to grief after a fire at sea.

There wasn't much time to get more than the essence of the places we visited – like the bustling, lime-white city of Jerusalem with its churches, its temples, its rich-coloured markets, its crowded streets, high wailing wall and its inherent history. I found small things mind-blowing – a white signpost with the name Bethlehem just as if it had been Errol. Were we really near to this place that had been a bright light in my imagination for all these years. Did it really exist? But when we got there I found it quite easy to imagine the stable as it had been even although the supposed site is now gaudily furnished and lit by many thin tapering candles. Back on the cruise ship, after a dark night's sail to Egypt, and a long journey in a convoy of coaches with an armed guard, we came to Cairo and to some of the famous pyramids on the outskirts of that city, sited far closer to the urban centre than I had imagined.

One year we went to southern Spain. While there we took the train from Alicante to Denia several times just to see the aquamarine sea on one side and the rocky ochre-yellow mountains on the other.

Another year we went to Greece – down south to the

Pelopenese to a small coastal resort with a cerulean bay not far from Mycenae. How well I remember the journey there through the night in a rattling bus that shook our innards to pieces. At two o'clock in the morning we stopped at Corinth and disembarked. A Grecian moon, the shape of a perfect pearl, was turning an ancient eucalyptus tree to silver. In the opalescent light I looked down into the incredible canal. There was a ship way down at the bottom, looking unreal – an ethereal ghost ship and I wondered, as I had done as a child on seeing a ship in a bottle, how it had ever got there, the sides of the canal being so high and close together. Hours later, an enormous crimson sun rose from the sea as we rounded the bend into our destination – Tolo.

The following year we got a little bolder and booked to go to an unexplored-by- tourist part of Turkey. We were enchanted by its high mountains and turquoise rivers tumbling down the steep slopes. We were captivated by the many ancient ruined towns and temples still uncommercialised and with pieces of ancient artefacts lying around at random – a finger carved out of marble, a bunch of grapes, a cluster of flowers, a reptile. There were also the weedy and wild-flowered, wide, terraced steps of amphitheatres – so many that we began to bemoan "not another amphitheatre". Rounding a river bend one day we came on hundreds of terrapins basking in the sun on top of a green film of algae. Our shadows fell across them. They disappeared with the speed of light through the green surface which closed up immediately as if nothing had ever touched it. Turkey was very different to any place we had been before, seeing the women all dressed in long flowing trousers and being wakened by the muesims calling the faithful to prayer at an unearthly hour in the morning.

A newspaper advert encouraged us to venture further. Trailfinders were offering cheap flights round the world. We had always, at the back of our minds, the thought that one day we would go to visit the parents of Richard's wife, Linda. Often they had urged us to come. Here was our opportunity and to go round the world as well. We flew to Boston stayed there a night and then went to Detroit to catch the plane for Australia. It was a long and tedious flight, the most memorable event being when, just as the sun rimmed the horizon, we saw though the cabin window the unmistakable cone of Mount Fugiyama suffused in pink light.

Australia was a leap in the imagination I hadn't expected. Linda's kind parents met us at dawn at Sydney airport and in three weeks stay there took us around everywhere they could think of. I was impressed by downtown Sydney, its colourful, high-rise castles of glass, its street canyons, its harbour, its opera house and by the impressive blue mountains not so far off covered in endless miles of eucalyptus trees. We flew up to Cairns – a totally different place. Here we found all the tropical islands rolled into one. We took a trip to Green Island – in a ferry filled with Japanese honeymooners – went on a semi submersible to get a close-up view of the incredible coral and coloured fish. It was on Green Island that we met a Texan in a broad-brimmed hat. We talked to him in the shade of palm trees over a cup of iced tea. At one point I moaned about losing a day because of crossing time zones on our way here. He told me he had also.

"But you will get it back because you are going back the same way as you came. We're going round the world – we won't!"

"You'll just have to have that one out with God!" was his reply

After Australia we stopped off in Manila in the Philippines – again a completely different experience. We met up with a most obliging taxi man who for very little money took us everywhere he could think of in the three days we were there. He showed us Manila with its palaces and poverty. We wanted to get out of Manila – get an idea of the countryside. This was not so easy. Manila stretches for miles and is jammed with cars and brightly coloured jeepneys which are used as mini buses. The taxi man had rarely been out of Manila himself so together it became an adventure to see the lush countryside with market stalls laden with exotic fruit and vegetables at intervals along the road. We saw how the people lived – the oxen that worked the land. We watched men climb with ease up tall palms to harvest the coconuts in much the same way as they had always done. We saw neat and clean children walk home from school often barefooted. We saw lakes and islands and homes in the shadow of an active volcano that might erupt at any time.

Next stop was Bangkok in Thailand. A big modern city, to a large extent, except when you got among the golden temples. We went further afield and sailed up the River Kwai to where on one bank above the river a huge golden Bhudda sat in the sun smiling at us. Afterwards Abadabi and home.

Several years later Trailfinders were still advertising cheap trips round the world.

"What about it?" I said to Henry one evening. "What about New Zealand this time. Around the world again but going the other way. Remember that Texan who told us to get our lost day back we would just have to have it out with God. Well, don't let's chance it. Let's do something about it – God helps those who help themselves."

We booked the trip.

But there was one place that perhaps I wanted to visit, go back to more than anywhere else and that was Canada. I wanted to see Alberta again and the places we had once lived all these years ago and I wanted to travel further north and see above all Canada's North West Territories and Lindberg's Landing that I had heard so much about from Grant. But that would have to be another trip.

Chapter 38

The Start of the Long Trail

It was a busy time for me when *Far from the Rowan Tree* was published. There were launches, readings, talks, interviews with newspapers. I was amazed at the interest. In Scotland it was selling well. In Perthshire very well. In the local Perth paper, it stayed at the top of the book charts for five months running. By Spring the first edition was almost sold out. I had not dreamed it would be so popular. The publisher also had distribution in Canada and I toyed with the idea of going over there – going round the bookstores, getting myself known, but thought it would be too expensive and a bore for Henry. However round about Christmas time Henry looked up from a newspaper he was reading.

"It'll soon be 1998," he said, "a hundred years since the Trail of the '98, – the year of the gold rush in the Yukon. I'd love to go to Alaska! When I was in Canada twenty years ago I nearly made it but not quite. I was working way up on the Alaska highway for a time. Helping on the roadworks. I never made it to Skagway where so many men from every walk of life began the long trek to the goldfields in the Yukon – all with gold fever. I saw a picture once of a long line of them going over the Chillcoot pass. One after another struggling over that mountain with heavy packs – never forgotten it. After that they still had a long way to go in a hostile, cold, uninhabited country – making their own canoes to cross vast lakes, living rough, very rough, then reaching Whitehorse to journey six hundred miles up the Yukon River. I've always wanted to see that part of the world – go there one day."

There was a pause while he turned another page. The logs in the wood-burning stove cracked and flared up. Outside the window, in the dark beyond the old velvet curtains, wind

199

whipped into a fury and then Henry said, "It'll soon be the year of the '98 again. What better year to go there?"

"You don't really mean it," I said. "How on earth would we get there? It would be terribly expensive."

"Not really," he explained. "It's a good exchange rate just now. We could fly to Vancouver – spend a week or so visiting the friends and relations we've got on Salt Spring Island, Vancouver Island and Powell River. Come back to Vancouver and pick up a camper van. Hire it for four weeks perhaps. That should be long enough." The seed of an idea began to form in my mind.

> "a hundred years since the Trail of the '98, – the year of the gold rush in the Yukon – what better year to go there?"

"Would it be possible also to visit Grant's old place, Lindberg's Landing?"

"Don't know why not – there's a road in there now – Grant helped to finish it."

"Afterwards we can go back to Edmonton and visit all our old haunts. Fly home perhaps from Edmonton or Calgary."

"And I could visit book shops in the bigger towns."

"Why not?" Quickly a route was beginning to take shape.

"It's an awful long way to drive but we could share the driving," I said.

"I've driven these roads before. They are bound to be a lot better now – nothing to it. We'll stay at camp sites. Grant says there's quite a lot of them nowadays."

I could see Henry was as keen if not more keen than I was to do the trip.

We set about finding the cheapest way and got £700 off the bill by going to a direct company found in the Yellow Pages rather than a travel agent. We booked for five weeks, flying to Vancouver and returning from Calgary, a thousand miles or so distant across the Rockies. The company sent us a brochure. From its pages we chose the smallest camper van. We would pick it up in Vancouver, deposit it at the firm's depot in Calgary on the day we would leave Canada to fly home. We chose May as the best month to travel. The ice should have broken up in the lakes and rivers by then and we hoped it would be before the hatching out of mosquitoes and flies.

"Are you sure we're not too old to be going on this kind of adventure," I said to Henry one evening after everything had been arranged.

"Not a bit of it. You're just as old as you feel and I feel around thirty."

We had a productive and happy time on the islands. On Salt Spring we spent a couple of happy days with Sheila and her Hungarian husband. Sheila and I had done our nurses' training when young together and had always kept in touch. She now lived in what I called paradise – in a house built of logs, a hidden retreat of woodland. Spring had come, humming birds were back. Her husband Andrew's great love was rhododendrons. He had around two hundred different species growing in the forest. He treated them with the greatest of care. Quite a few of them were in bloom when we were there. Beautiful heads in the softest yellow, richest red, most delicate mauve. They were difficult to protect here, what with visiting deer and beavers and, most troublesome of all, the weather. In Victoria we stayed with old friends who had helped us when we were poor immigrants in Edmonton all those years ago. Gordon, the husband, after he retired, brought out a writing magazine which he kept going for ten years. He couldn't have been more helpful towards me and my book. He took me to all the bookstores he could think of and explained how to go about things. I needn't have been nervous about approaching these bookstores – they were all most helpful and interested.

Next port of call was to a niece in Qualicum Beach – a warm-hearted niece who lived in a wooden house surrounded by six acres of land. Her sister happened to be staying there also for a week which saved us from having to go to Powell River. They were interested in our forthcoming expedition. Although they had lived in that part of the world for most of their lives, they had never been to the Yukon or to Alaska.

"Are you sure you'll be okay? A small camper did you say?"

"Yes we've chosen the smallest one in the brochure."

"I didn't think we had small anything in this part of the world." She left it at that, but made the same offer as Sheila, my friend in Salt Spring had a day or two earlier, "Get into any sort of difficulty. We're here to help. Just phone."

After a week we crossed over to Vancouver and had a cheerful time with a brother-in-law and family. Next morning we were ready to go and made our way to where we were to pick up our camper.

We got a taxi to take us there. The taxi-driver had a bit of trouble finding the place but we were pleased to note it was on the outskirts of Vancouver and in the direction we wanted to go. I had been worrying quietly for some time. How do you get a vehicle you are not familiar with out of a city you are not familiar with.

We entered into a huge shed. A man walking on stilts was painting an enormously tall wall. Ranged along the opposite side were a row of the tallest campers I have ever seen. To me, that morning in that shed, they looked enormous. Across the top of each in big scrawling letters was Rocky Mountain Campers. My heart sank. I looked around. I could see nothing smaller. Surely they didn't expect us to drive one of these monsters. But that's just what they did. We sat down opposite the guy at the desk. I looked at Henry. He didn't say anything but I could see the corners of his mouth had drooped. Always so confident, that was not a good sign.

"Have you nothing smaller?" I said. "We did order the smallest one in the brochure."

"That's it," said the man.

"Do you not have anything else?"

"Nope."

What about a car? We could stay at motels.

"Nope, don't have a car either. 'Fraid that's our little lot."

Well if it was that or nothing, we couldn't draw back now. Out came all the forms – all the rules and regulations. It all seemed straight forward enough until we came to rule 26. Clients can't take the camper into the Yukon, Alaska or Northwest Territories.

Here Henry stopped him. "But that's exactly where we're heading for. It was all arranged over the phone. We were definitely told we could go there. We would not have hired the camper had we been told otherwise. Anyway why this regulation?"

"I guess it is because the roads are a bit dodgy up there. Campers that go there tend to come back covered in dents from flying gravel and with their windscreens all pitted."

"Well what do we do now?" I said despairingly. "We don't really need a camper if we can't go there."

"I'll see what I can do," said the fellow. He left and there was much discussion with a colleague. After a few phone calls, he was back at the desk.

"The company's decided that you folks can go to these places seeing as how you were misinformed but you'll need to pay us $300 extra." There was nothing else we could do – we agreed. He continued with the rules all about what to do if we had an accident.

"Now when you guys have an accident," he said.

"Surely you mean, if," I said.

After the form-filling and various extra payments we were ready to go but by now other customers were waiting to be seen. Our young man was in a hurry. Our monster was brought out and we were shown, in a matter of minutes, how everything worked. Impossible to take it all in. We asked about a manual of instructions but there was none. We were given a small map showing how to get out of Vancouver and he quickly explained what further roads to take to reach Hope, our first destination.

In spite of the excitement and confusion, all might have gone well had we not missed an important junction. I saw it, but too late. We were in the wrong lane and passed helplessly by. We took two more hours to get out of the busy suburb of Vancouver called Langley. At one point the Rocky Mountain Campers man's prediction "When you have an accident" very nearly came true. We came to a busy intersection and did something we shouldn't have done. (I still don't know what, but their traffic rules are different from ours.) A stretch limousine came winging down, much faster than it should have done, and had almost to go sideways to miss us. All the traffic stopped in fright and let us go where we were heading for.

If the rest of the traffic got a fright it was nothing to what we got. Henry manoeuvred into a side road and ran the camper onto a bank. It slipped back onto the road. Where was the hand brake? On the floor. Henry wasn't accustomed to driving an automatic. Everything about it was different. To make matters worse the rain had come on heavily. How did the windscreen wipers work? During our rest on the bank however we managed to work out most things and started again. We still had trouble getting on to the proper trail, when all of a sudden I saw it for the second time. We were in the wrong lane again. There was no way we could see what was behind us. The camper was so wide that even the extra long mirrors gave you no view to speak of.

Henry indicated – dared to move over. At last we were on our way.

Chapter 39
Riding the Alaska Highway

After that first frightening beginning things went well enough. We drew into the camp site at Hope in the late afternoon. We had hamburgers at a nearby restaurant and then explored our first Canadian campsite, pretty among trees. We began to learn the language – the dumping station for getting rid of waste – the electricity for boosting supplies – the water supply for filling up Camper tanks of which we had three – one for drinking water; one for dish washing; one for the shower and lavatory. They held a lot of water and were situated at the top of the vehicle.

"All that water on the top," said Henry, "makes it difficult to drive. It gives it a swaying motion just like a ship at sea!" Later we kept the tanks low in water. The camper itself was comfortable – everything one could wish. We climbed up onto our double bed that night and fell asleep easily. We had no feeling of claustrophobia as the ceiling was so high. Also the van was new. It had done only 600 miles.

"At least we won't be in too much danger of breaking down when we are out in the barren lands," Henry said optimistically.

We got to sleep all right but staying asleep was a little more difficult. At regular intervals trains passed. They seemed to be just on our doorstep and waiting till they reached us before letting off their loud and mournful whistles – the mountains that were close echoed the sound which made it go on for ever.

In the morning in glorious sunshine, we got a proper look at those mountains that rose so close to us. We could hardly believe them. Last night they had been shrouded in mist and rain. Today they were standing clear and bright. They went straight up into the blue sky. We were almost too near to see the tops.

This was to be our introduction to the incredible journey up

205

the Alaska highway. I have to admit that for the first day or two as much of my attention was given to the white line on my side of the road as to the quite magnificent scenery of mountains, canyons and rivers.

"You're too near the white line," was my constant cry. Henry would pull over a fraction. All the way up, the road had a sloping shoulder if not a precipice at my side. If the camper had gone too far to the right it would have been well and truly stuck, if not worse. Henry's problem was that juggernauts kept passing on the other side with what seemed like inches to spare and we had very limited vision behind. By about the third day I began to relax and enjoy this truly magnificent Alaska trail. Once we got out of the spectacular Fraser Canyon country with its rivers, lakes, gorges, mountains and trees, we drifted into the Caribou. Here the scenery was completely different. It was ranch country – a lot of horses around and the occasional attractive ranch house – still lonely but full of interest. The road was good, the sun was shining, we were happy.

I had taken an anthology of Canadian poetry, chosen with the help of our friend Gordon in Victoria.

"All the best Canadian poets from early on," he'd told me. I'd promised to give a talk on Canadian poetry in England when I got back before realising I didn't know all that much about it.

For me the long days with Henry at the wheel (I never plucked up the courage to drive the thing) were spent just watching and being thrilled by the spectacular scenery. From time to time I would nod off, or read poems that often related to the wild terrain we were passing through. And there was that white line.

The second night was spent parked at the water's edge of a lonely and still lake – a camping site with no one else there but us. It had a fresh and primordial feel to it. The grass was fresh green, the trees were all coming into leaf, Spring birds were singing and as the spectacular sunset faded there arose a cry I knew of old. From across the water the eerie mechanical laughter of a Loon.

Next day we took a detour off the Alaska trail – the secondary road looked as if it would be a more direct route to our destination for that night. It was a beautiful road and very scenic.

We rounded a bend and suddenly a school and a 30ks sign. We were driving faster than that. I shouted to Henry – I knew he hadn't noticed – too late – a mounty's car sat at the side of the road – a spider waiting to catch flies. The signs had just been put up. Would they be obeyed? We weren't quite sure if it was a cop car, slowed down but carried on.

"It's turning," I said to Henry.

"Perhaps it's nothing to do with us. We'll soon know."

I expected it to draw in front of us with flashing lights at any moment but no – nothing, and then I heard the sirens. Henry being a wee bit deaf didn't hear them.

"Pull in Henry," I said, "or we will be in trouble." Henry veered into the side and stopped. We didn't have to wait long. A mounty was at our window.

"we hadn't driven very far from the township when I saw my first bear – it was very black and running down a mountain side just as casually as a cat would cross a carpet"

"You guys not see me behind you?"

"No," said Henry politely and truthfully and explained about the mirrors. They weren't our fault. We had tried to extend them further. They were at their fullest reach.

The mounty examined them saw our problem but said little about that.

"You guys realise you were exceeding the speed limit for a school zone."

Henry apologised and said he did not.

"Where you guys from anyway?"

"Scotland." Whereupon we were told of his Scottish forebears and a lot else besides.

At one point Henry said, "Seems we took a wrong turning coming this way."

"Not at all," said the mounty. "You took the right turn. This is the most scenic route in all of Canada."

He let us drive on after about an hour of chat. Very kindly let us off with a warning. "I could fine you $150," he said. Instead he gave us his card.

"Just you be careful. You guys are kinda lucky. You've got the road up north kinda quiet this early in the season. Next weekend all sorts of vehicles going up north after winter."

In the end I was glad we did take the detour because we hadn't driven very far from the township when I saw my first bear. I couldn't quite believe it. It was very black and running down a precipitous and greening mountain side just as casually as a cat would cross a carpet.

Next day we started off to cross Steamboat Mountain.

"What a picturesque name," I said to Henry once we got underway.

"I remember it of old," he said. "Always rather an obstacle to get over in the old days but should be okay now. This road has changed. I just don't recognise it. It was truly just a trail forty odd years ago. Now it's a good modern road and used a lot, by the looks of it."

He was wrong about Steamboat Mountain being easy. I wondered why it was called the Steamboat but as we approached it became not quite such a mystery – a thick mist that could have passed as steam enveloped most of it. Heavy rain came on and there was not much traffic as we began to ascend. The road was steep with lots of bends and the surface was greasy. As we climbed, with one or two cars in front and one behind, things got worse and worse. The road was under construction but today all equipment was abandoned. Graders lay askew everywhere – a look of desertion about.

The rain lashed down. At one point flood water had completely washed away the side of the road – there was just enough room to pass. I closed my eyes. It was terrifying. I forgot all about the white lines after that – they became insignificant. We followed my leader down that great mountain. There was nothing else we could do other than go on.

At the first opportunity we stopped at a rest area. Our camper was unrecognisable. Where was our beautiful new gleaming cream van with the blue Rocky Mountain scrawled across its high top. It now had a thin layer of mud all over.

Next day, on calling in at a gas station to refuel the enormous tank the attendant said, "You guys must have come over the Steamboat yesterday. You've sure got your van in a mess. Still you were lucky. Had to rescue a fellow there yesterday. He slipped down a slope – what a mess his vehicle was in but he was okay."

Further on in our trip a driver of a juggernaut pulled into a rest area near the Great Slave Lake. We got to talking.

"How was your journey?"

We talked of the Steamboat. He had crossed over with his juggernaut on the same day and had got stuck up to the axles.

Chapter 40

The Yukon and Alaska

After the Steamboat Henry was in an area he remembered well. He had worked for some time on the Alaska highway in the Muncho Lake district all those years ago.

He had forgotten just how beautiful it was in its snow-capped mountain setting – a still lake a long lonely way from any town, shining in the sun, now jade, now torquoise, now cerulean.

The weather improved and was perfect by the time we reached Liard Springs, where we stopped for the night. Next day we would be in the Yukon. As far as campsites were concerned Liard Springs was unique. It had hot springs. In the cool evening air we could see the steam rising as we approached. A big campsite, it was as yet half empty and each camper van had a tree-lined bay to itself. Opposite our one stood a big pump which gushed out water, the few campers keeping it in constant use.

The evenings here were long. It was almost midnight before it grew dark. Birdsong was heard till late. One bird in particular, the one I had first heard at the lake with the loons, was to haunt me all the way north. It sang its heart out from the top of a tree and was answered by its mate. It was almost dark before it stopped singing, to begin again at first light. Several hundred yards away from our bay was a board walk made of slats of wood that led over a marsh. Here pools of water gave an occasional bubble. There were lots of birds of all kinds in the marshland quite close to us. I could have stood and watched them for hours. Over on the other side was a deep pool from which steam was rising. Campers were in bathing. I felt the water. It was hot hot.

Don't go far to the right I was told. It's too hot. Further up there was a hanging garden. A great wild rockery holding small pools of warm water. Rare flowers grew here. Wild animals were to be seen in this campsite too and everywhere there were signs – A FED BEAR IS A DEAD BEAR.

Bears don't often attack you, I'd been told, especially not black bears – it's rare but I'd heard too many instances of attack to think it was quite rare enough. Someone told me later that only the year before, two children had been mauled in this campsite and their father who went to their rescue was mauled too. I didn't ask further.

I could hardly believe, next day, that I was in the Yukon. To begin with, it wasn't so very different from the northern British Columbia that we travelled through. What had I expected? – perhaps some of the scenes that Robert W. Service depicted in his poems. At Watson Lake we stopped at a modern township to get provisions.

Our objective that night was to reach Teslin. We made it and parked in a bare campsite with very few trees beside the wide Teslin river still half covered in ice – a shining silver – northern-looking – more what I had expected – beautiful in a lonely far-north way. Just beside the campsite was the bridge by which we had crossed the river – it had shuggled and rattled when we crossed. All night it rattled with traffic crossing.

Next day we were in Whitehorse. I have to confess being disappointed in Whitehorse. What did I expect – something out of Robert W. Service again?. But Whitehorse is a modern city with wide streets and handsome shops and restaurants. We arrived first, down beside the Yukon River. Here the old paddle steamer, *Klondike*, is on show. It's been preserved just as it was when it made the long journey up the Yukon River to Dawson City. It was so well preserved I could feel I was back at the end of the nineteenth century. The high holds held all the goods that would have been carried at that time. On one deck we were shown the cabins and dining room used by rich passengers who wanted to travel to Dawson City. Very elegant it all looked with small tables covered in white cloths and laid with shining cutlery. The *Klondike* used to travel up regularly with prospectors and provisions, and later well-heeled passengers, for Dawson City. On the return journey it was heavily laden with silver ore.

At Whitehorse Henry and I had to come to a decision. We had originally intended to travel as far north as Dawson City. That was another six hundred miles and back. We had taken longer than anticipated to reach this far. Skagway in Alaska, where we also wanted to go, was a lot nearer and we really didn't think we had time to go to both.

Henry said, "I'd rather visit Skagway. More than anything else I want to see where those would-be miners landed and get to feel the country they had to traverse before they got to Dawson City – that great mountain pass they had to cross before reaching the Yukon River."

So Skagway it was. We set off from Whitehorse on a day of bright blue skies. Some of the highest of the Rocky Mountains are in the Yukon and the lakes really have to be seen to be believed. The colours are exquisite. No painter could adequately catch them – no poet tell in words, however skilled. Emerald Lake in particular took my breath away – what fantastic depth of colour – and no one there – no one at all but us.

Soon we entered what in the brochures is called 'mountains of the moon' country – breathtakingly barren and out of this world. The sky clouded over – the snow began to fall – I began to worry again. What if we were snowed up in this God-forsaken spot? Arrival at U.S. Customs proved a distraction.

We had to show our passports etc, and pay twelve dollars to be allowed into Alaska – and at last in another magic-in-my-imagination place. It wasn't long till we were descending out of the mountains down a precipitous slope that fell away very steeply into a deep gorge. The sheer impact of it was somewhat diffused by crash barriers for most of the way, for which I, and probably many another traveller, was most thankful.

If Whitehorse had disappointed, Skagway achieved the opposite. It was preserved very much as it had been – the old shacks still around and anything new, built in the old style – the effect was perfect. It wasn't big, a one horse kind of a town but with plenty of restaurants and shops. Its harbour, on the other hand, was big and in the season is the berthing place of huge cruise liners, sometimes as many as four at a time. They come on certain days of the week when the whole town is populated with strangers. It had always been thus, ever since the gold mining days.

We arrived on a day when no cruise liners were in. It was very quiet. At the station which was close to our campsite we bought tickets for the train ride up the mountain. The railroad had been built for the prospectors at the beginning of the century. Had I known what the journey would be like, I would never have entertained it. Quite the most frightening train journey I have ever made. The track went up the side of the gorge and took us to within sight of the White Pass. The gorge bottom looked very very far down – the valley where thousands upon thousands of horses had died in the early days of the goldrush.

"If a rock crashes down from the mountain – at it looks as if one could at any moment – what would happen if the train crashed into it ?" asked a man sitting in front of me.

It didn't dare think about it and worse was to come. Nearing the top we had to cross one of these old spidery bridges made of wood. It didn't look strong enough to take the weight of the train, and it looked ancient. We got across all right and saw the desolate White Pass all covered in snow.

"What a place – what men – what they went through – what bravery all in the cause of gold," Henry had felt the tremendous essence of it for himself.

In the evening we went to a show similar to those put on for the prospectors all those years ago. First a recital of the works of Robert W. Service for any who cared to come early. I could have wished for no better. The old-timer in his wide-brimmed stetson, complete with guitar, performed to perfection. Then the show – the honky tonk piano, the not too slim girls in gaudy flared skirts and black garters doing the can-can – everything about the show evoked some of the aura of the goldrush years, even the stage exit being a door opening out onto the wooden boardwalk of the township.

Next day the small town was filled to the gunwales with people – the cruise liners were in.

Chapter 41

A Pilgrimage Made

After Skagway came our long journey back. We had gone as far as we dared in the time available. Going back through border control into the Yukon was a much easier affair. The smiling Canadian came out to meet us – asked to see our passports and handed them back smiling – no forms to fill up – or money to hand over.

"Have a good day folks."

Back we went over the mountains of the moon again. Desolate country but not quite so frightening as the snow had stopped – the skies were a brilliant blue and what snow had fallen danced with white light in the sunshine. We didn't have to go all the way back to Whitehorse to get on the Alaska highway. There was a turn-off before the town.

We came to a small township. Flat-roofed houses scattered in wide space – a disused bit of railway line – a few delapidated cars and trucks in untidy heaps of rusting iron. It boasted a grocery and restaurant. We turned into its dusty streets – no one about. The mediocre-looking restaurant had a big Open sign in the window as had the cobwebbed window of the grocery store – no one about. We travelled on a bit further and came to a fork in the road.

"This way," I said to Henry not being quite sure . Twenty miles further on I was not at all sure. It was a very lonely road indeed. No traffic passed, there were few signs of habitation. We stopped and had a look at the map.

"I think it's right enough," said Henry. I was still full of doubt.

"Tell you what – the next place of any kind we'll stop and ask."

We came to a signpost – "Whispering Ranch" it said. We bounced down a very stony road for a mile or two always thinking we would come to a habitation. The road got stonier and stonier – there was a narrow stream to cross. Trees seemed to go on and on for ever. A black bear came out from the forest and ambled across our path.

"Let's turn," I said. "This is getting us nowhere." That was easier said than done, what with the narrow rocky road and the cumbersome camper.

When we got back to the end of the road I said, "Let's turn back – what if it's the wrong way and we end up somewhere where there is no gas – what then?" Henry wasn't pleased with this idea of retracing our route, but complied.

Back on the road to Whitehorse again we noticed a small attractive cabin on one side. It was freshly painted and neat as ninepence in the middle of nowhere. It advertised food and newly baked bread. We turned off into its small car park. Everywhere there were fluttering, brightly painted mechanical birds whirring in the slight breeze. We tinged open the cabin door. A waft from newly-baked fresh bread met us. A very stout lady came with a menu. We gave her an order – Blueberry pie and 7-Up. With no one else about we got into conversation. She told us of her love for the Yukon. She wasn't a native but had lived here for thirty years.

"Have you been further North?" she asked. "Been on the Demster highway?"

"No," we said.

"Ah, you haven't lived – what a road – it's like being on the top of the world."

Her words fired me into wanting to see more of the North land but we'd run out of time, not roads.

While we were there in the cabin with its pink and white table decoration, table cloths more like an English tea-room than somewhere in the Yukon, we asked directions.

"You've been on the right enough road," she said philosophically, "but it was good you came back, you met me!" From anyone else that might have seemed an immodest statement.

We retraced our wheelmarks and eventually came to the end of that long lonely road. We had the bonus of seeing another black bear at the road verge, a caribou and a wolf.

Another two days on the Alaska highway again and we approached Fort Nelson and our turn-off point. The road was busier now – the same amount of juggernauts but more cars and more of the enormous vehicles so many Americans call home. They were no higher or wider than our camper but were twice as long – as long as a bus and trailing a car behind them.

Americans making their way up to Alaska. We had met some of them on our way up at the rest areas. After a long time on the road they were always pleased to talk. They all had much the same story. They had once worked in Alaska, had relations or friends there, had given up their homes, bought a home on wheels and lived a gypsy sort of existence but with all the mod cons. They all seemed happy people. We enjoyed their company. One American disappeared into his travelling house while we chatted to his wife and came out with a large sealed jar. "Smoked salmon," he said, "for you."

The Liard highway leading to Lindberg's Landing branches off some way before Fort Nelson. However we felt we must go back to Fort Nelson, to the liquor store and get Ed some whisky which we knew he liked.

I could hardly believe we were on the Liard highway. Here we were on the road that Grant had helped to build. Long and lonely we'd been warned – watch out for wandering bison. By the time we reached Fort Liard the tank was running low. We turned into this township whose few houses straggled haphazardly for a mile or so and found the gas station and the restaurant. It was a help yourself. Henry put the gas pipe into the tank – a hollow woosh – nothing, empty. We had to get gas. The young first nation girl attendant shrugged her shoulders – "Gas tank come – maybe half an hour."

We couldn't think where it could possibly come from in that time but we would have to wait till it came even if it took two days. Two hours later it appeared. In the meantime we went to the restaurant. No one came to serve us. We went to the counter and asked for coffee. A young girl appeared and pointed to an almost hidden coffee maker. We were supposed to take our own. We bought a couple of packets of crisps – the only food we could see around. In the end the girl smiled and gave us the coffee free.

Out on the road again with a full tank we felt better. It seemed to wind on endlessly – there was little traffic, just forest and now and again, wild animals – a black bear, a martin whisking across a stretch of tarmac, and then an enormous bison grazing by the roadside in the evening air, quite unconcerned by our passing. Not long after we had seen the bison we came to a rest area. There weren't many on this road. So as we were hungry we pulled in to make our evening meal.

Henry took a look out to see how thick the mosquitoes were. "Good heavens, what do we do now, Margaret? Come and have a look."

I looked out of the back screen door. There, yards away was a bison grazing.

"I'm certainly not moving till it's gone," I said somewhat overcome by the monstrous size of its shoulders.

"It could easily knock over the van if it wanted to," Henry said.

We sat in trepidation for a while but the enormous beast moved on, unconcerned, grazing as it went.

It wasn't too much longer till we got to the Blackstone – the recreation park that Grant had helped to create. It was all that Grant said and more – a natural, green place down by the Liard river. Each of its forty tree-lined bays a delight. It was 8pm and there was no one, just no one, about. We had all of its forty bays to choose from and opted for a secluded hollow on the banks of the river – a mistake, the mosquitoes homed in on us. But I didn't care. I was here – the place I thought I would never be – the place in the wilderness Grant had helped to make. Right now it seemed as if we were the only people in the world.

It wasn't too long, however before the roar of a motor bike shattered the silent air and a young first nation lad appeared on our doorstep – sixteen dollars for the night. He was a polite young fellow. We invited him in away from the cloud of mosquitoes. We talked a while, said we knew the Lindbergs. Were they far off?

"Quite close, going there now," he said and gave us directions for the morning.

"I suppose he'll tell them we're here," I said to Henry. "Pity.

I had wanted to make it a complete surprise and just arrive on their doorstep."

And that's what we did next morning. And that's what it was – a complete surprise – the young fellow hadn't mentioned it.

They didn't even guess who we were, but there were hugs all round when we told them. What a warm welcome. I couldn't quite believe it – the place I thought I would never see – the people I thought I might never meet, and here we were.

Ed Lindberg was very much as I imagined he would be – a big rangy man with strong broad shoulders, outgoing, enthusiastic, enterprising – a friend to the whole world. Sue Lindberg was rather a surprise. I hadn't expected a tall, slim, pretty, elegant lady of Swiss descent. Warm-hearted and kind I knew she would be. We stayed for a weekend there in their little bit of wilderness.

We ate moose meat and caribou, pike from the river and vegetables from the root cellar – all grown in their few short months of summer and stored. The potatoes were big and beautiful and it was nearly June. They were last year's and still firm. Ed and Sue couldn't do enough for us.

We were shown over their settlement which was now large. They had recently bought over their only neighbour's property. They had quite a few cabins complete with root cellars. From local timber they had built themselves a large new ranch-style house beside the river. Just as at Inchmichael, the large kitchen was the heart of the home. The world, once travelling by river but now as often by road, was entertained there. The Lindbergs had difficulties getting to the outside world but it didn't seem to matter. The world came to them.

Quite a few visitors came while we were there but you felt, with Susan, there would never be too many to feed. Now I understood why Grant had stayed here so long. It was a home from home and Sue cared about little things. Some chickens had hatched just before we arrived. One was sickly. Sue had it in a warm oven to see if it would survive. She was doubtful but I thought it would – it was tr ying so very hard. That chicken was brought out on the table and encouraged to pick at tiny crumbs and drink from a saucer. I heard later, by letter, that it had survived. Sue and I had a lot in common.

Being shown round the property was fantastically interesting to us, seeing all the things that Grant had told us about – the cabins in the forest, the wooden cachés on stilts to store food away from the bears, the deep-down root cellars, the saws with which Grant had worked and best of all perhaps for Henry the idle gold dredger that really would be able to take gold out of the Liard, had Ed the time to get round to it.

We slept in the camper at night outside the veranda of their house. Midnight and it was barely dark – almost the land of the midnight sun, now it was almost June. I lay listening to the silence broken only by that bird that had haunted me all the way north, with its perfect primeaval notes. Here it sang louder and clearer than ever epitomising wilderness. *Pi peep, pi peep, pi* rang through the midnight air – all joy and hope sustained in these simple notes. Only a short time elapsed till it sang again as the pale dawn glowed into day.

I asked Sue about the bird next morning.

"I'm not quite sure," she said. "I'm so accustomed to the bird, I've never really questioned. I think it must sing all night. Perhaps it's the white-throated sparrow.

It seemed too prosaic a name for a bird that poured its heart out in such clear pure tones.

What's in a name? I thought.

Chapter 42
Old Haunts

Rather than retrace our tyre marks, when we left Lindberg's Landing we followed the Liard highway until it met with the McKenzie highway further north. Near the junction there was a lonely gas station – no more for around two hundred miles. We filled the tank to the very brim and headed south. Thirty five miles in the opposite direction was the ferry that took people to Fort Simpson. I would love to have gone there – the township on the other side of the Liard after which came unpopulated hinterland all the way to the Arctic Circle. I didn't mention this to Henry. We had a long enough journey ahead of us for a day and Henry, I knew, would have gone to please me.

The McKenzie highway proved to be the loneliest road we had ever been on. There was hardly any traffic, save for a truck or two passing in a cloud of dust. The good road surface just seemed to go on for ever into the endless horizons that shimmered in the distance. Surely round the next corner (and there wasn't even many of these) there would be a house, a building of some kind. But there was nothing the eye could see, only dark scrub fir trees lining the road that had a broad verge of well-kept green as a firebreak. It was rather like some great Lord's drive up to a castle but there was no castle and you could see neither through the trees nor over the trees – nothing to break the monotony. There was the occasional road sign that said, Buckle Up, or Emergency Airstrip where the road ballooned out, or a slowly decreasing number of ks still to go to the next settlement called Enterprise.

Half way there however, much to our surprise, there was a new-looking campsite. We went in – no gas but somewhere you could get a cup of coffee – a tourist office, would you believe, all very modern and state-of-the-art and silent and strange. There was a woman there in a cabin half-hidden in the trees. She was hanging out clothes – certainly not expecting any visitors. We walked down steps to the river – it was cool and silent apart from the Spring birds. Outside the entrance to the campsite, very black against the green sward of wayside grass was a mother bear with two inky-black cubs just to remind us we were in the wilderness.

Shortly before reaching Enterprise we pulled into a rest area and got out to stretch our legs. We looked over an incredible valley of trees to the widest of horizons. The sky was incredibly blue but along the horizon there was a strange band of white, straight, like a frieze bordering tree-green wallpaper.

"What's that?" I said to Henry.

"Must be cloud."

"No, it's not cloud – too regular."

Just then a juggernaut pulled in. The driver, a broad-shouldered, rugged fellow wearing a peaked cap and holding onto his thermos mug, jumped down from its high cab. We got talking. I asked about the strange horizon.

"Must be cloud," he said.

He took a second look. "I know what it is – never really noticed before – it's the ice on the Great Slave Lake. It's sure not all melted yet." It was the 1st of June. I wanted to see the Great Slave.

"How far is it?" I asked.

"Hay River," he said. "That's where it begins. Goes right up a hundred miles to Yellowknife.

Next day we went to Hay River for gas and to see the Great Slave Lake. It was a bigger place than I expected with modern buildings. We went down to the lake and spent a lovely sunny day there, the more enjoyable because of the absence of mosquitoes. The great shelf of ice wasn't far offshore but round the edges the water was blue as *lapis lasuli* and there were boys swimming and not shivering with cold. The next night we were heading for Edmonton.

On the way I wanted to take in Lake Nakamun – the lake that my late husband, Ronald had worked to open up all those years ago when we emigrated to Canada. It was a difficult place to find. It had been fairly simple in the old days when there weren't many roads to choose from. But now there was a grid of roads all numbered but unnamed, mostly serving the little cabins and farms – hobby farms, the owners having jobs as well.

At last we came on it by luck more than anything – a great big sign saying Camp Nakamun. We went up a well-kept drive to a green sward of close-cropped grass leading down to the lake. On top of the rise stood a big wooden lodge. We heard voices down at the lake. Young fellows with canoes politely told us it belonged to the Alliance of Churches and was a holiday camp for youth and for older people. We went through the enormous lounge furnished with easy chairs and found the warden drying dishes. We told him our mission and he immediately offered to take us a sail round the lake in a barge.

"The summer village of Nakamun," he pointed as we approached the opposite shore, "self-governing and rather exclusive." I saw the attractive cabins peeping through the trees as I tried to work out where we had been. That ancient wooden mansion on the rise – it was no longer there but a new one had taken its place. I tried to work out where the lots were that Ronald had sold for cabins.

"These very ancient cabins," said our host. "Oh there are very few of them left."

The words ancient struck me as odd. In some ways it seemed just like yesterday to me. I realised, all of a sudden, how time had moved on.

Our next stop was Wainwright, the township close to where we had lived and worked on a prairie farm all those years ago. I hardly recognised it, it had grown so. I had forgotten too how much oil there had been around this area. For a great part of the road from Vermillion to Wainwright there are these woodpecker oil pumps working. When we got to Wainwright there was no room at the inn – all three campsites were full with oil workers.

"We'll just journey on till we find one," Henry said. I looked up at the sky. Up till now the weather had been fine, but what I saw coming I immediately recognised. I may not have recognised much that I remembered about Wainwright, but this I did know – a great black anvil of cloud coming towards us – a storm. Quickly, the wind got up and we were in a cloud of dust. Lightening came in great streaks across the sky and thunder roared, followed by lashing rain.

"We're not going anywhere," I said. "We'll book into the motel for the night."

Next morning we visited the small museum down by the rail road. One of the first things I saw was a photograph of the Queen and her consort on the occasion of her visit to Wainwright thirty-five years ago. It brought back immediately to me that day we all went to see her there, waving to us from the back of the rail car.

That same day we headed for Edmonton. We had been told of the campsite down by the river and almost in the centre of town. In the busy traffic we began to go round in frightening circles reminiscent of Langley and drew into a MacDonalds which had a big parking area and calmed down over a bag of chips. A taxi drove past.

"Tell you what, Henry. How about hiring a taxi to lead us there?"

"Good idea," said Henry and so it proved to be. We got through the complicated streets no bother.

In Edmonton we got in contact with our first landlady who had been so kind to us all those years ago. Like me, her first husband had died and she had remarried. She and her husband were kindness itself. They fed us and took us around, back to where we had once lived. I remembered a pleasant avenue with attractive wooden houses all of different designs. Would it have changed? No, it hadn't changed much. The house we had lived in was no longer there but others were similar and trees and bushes had grown along the wide streets. I was not disappointed.

We stayed a day or two in Edmonton. I went to the main book shops. They were enthusiastic about *Far from the Rowan Tree* and got me to sign copies. We went to the University and were shown around by a pleasant young professor and poet to whom I had a letter of introduction.

The camper had to be at its destination by eleven o'clock on the day we were due to fly out of Calgary. We decided to take it a day early to leave time to find the place. The camper, despite all predictions back in Vancouver, had not one dent or chip. We had it washed – it was pristine clean – and only one useless wing mirror was missing.

Arriving in Calgary about eleven the next day, Henry suggested a train into town, visiting a bookstore, and returning by taxi. This might have been a great idea had we not left our all important bag with passports, air tickets, driving licences in the cab. It was off at speed just as we remembered.

Henry had the presence of mind to note name of the cab company. A taxi-driver from the same firm was helpfulness itself and eventually the missing essentials turned up at the police station.

That night we stayed in a hotel in one of Calgary's main streets. Next morning in brilliant sunlight we walked down the long pedestrian precinct. At the beautiful square at the bottom all was bright bustle, the Caribbean Canadians were having their Spring Carnival and were all changing into their brilliantly coloured clothes in the square. When it was ready we followed the lively procession dancing up the street. The music from the floats was such that those watching and following couldn't help but dance too. Me along with them. I'll never forget the dancing streets of Calgary, a suitable and moving end to an emotional journey.

At midnight we entered the silver bird to fly over the North Pole back to the fresh green fields of home, mission completed.